Unconventional Wisdom

Unconventional Wisdom

Counterintuitive Insights for Family Business Success

Edited by

John L. Ward

Wild Group Professor of Family Business
IMD – International Institute for Management
Development

Contributors

**Daniel Denison, Jean L. Kahwajy,
George Kohlrieser, Colleen Lief, Peter Lorange,
Joachim Schwass, Ulrich Steger**

John Wiley & Sons, Ltd

Other Wiley Editorial Offices

John Wiley & Sons Inc., 111 River Street, Hoboken, NJ 07030, USA

Jossey-Bass, 989 Market Street, San Francisco, CA 94103-1741, USA

Wiley-VCH Verlag GmbH, Boschstr. 12, D-69469 Weinheim, Germany

John Wiley & Sons Australia Ltd, 33 Park Road, Milton, Queensland 4064, Australia

John Wiley & Sons (Asia) Pte Ltd, 2 Clementi Loop #02-01, Jin Xing Distripark, Singapore 129809

John Wiley & Sons Canada Ltd, 22 Worcester Road, Etobicoke, Ontario, Canada M9W 1L1

Wiley also publishes its books in a variety of electronic formats. Some content that appears in print
may not be available in electronic books.

British Library Cataloguing in Publication Data

A catalogue record for this book is available from the British Library

ISBN-13 978-0-470-02165-1 (PB)
ISBN-10 0-470-02165-9 (PB)

Typeset in 10/16pt Kuenstler by Integra Software Services Pvt. Ltd, Pondicherry, India
Printed and bound in Great Britain by TJ International Ltd, Padstow, Cornwall, UK
This book is printed on acid-free paper responsibly manufactured from sustainable forestry in which
at least two trees are planted for each one used for paper production.

We are grateful to the 600 families who have shared their experiences with us during IMD's Leading the Family Business program from 1988 to 2004.

Contents

Contributors

Daniel Denison

Daniel Denison is Professor of Management and Organization at IMD. His research has shown a strong relationship between organizational culture and business performance metrics such as profitability, growth, customer satisfaction, and innovation. He has consulted with many leading corporations regarding organizational change, leadership development, and the cultural issues associated with mergers and acquisitions, turnarounds, and globalization. Dr Denison received his Bachelor's degree in psychology, sociology, and anthropology from Albion College and his PhD in organizational psychology from the University of Michigan.

Before joining IMD, Dr Denison was an Associate Professor of Organizational Behavior and Human Resource Management at the University of Michigan Business School, teaching in MBA, PhD, and executive education programs. He has taught and lived in Asia, Europe, Latin America, and the Middle East.

He has written several books, including *Corporate Culture and Organizational Effectiveness*, published by John Wiley in 1990. He is also the author of the *Denison Organizational Culture Survey* and the *Denison Leadership Development Surveys*. These surveys and the underlying models have been used by over 3000 organizations and are the basis of several ongoing research projects. His articles have appeared in a number of leading journals, including *The Academy of Management Review, Organization Science*, and *Policy Studies Review*.

Jean L. Kahwajy

Prior to joining IMD as Professor of Organizational Behavior, Dr Kahwajy worked as a coach, consultant, seminar leader, and speaker on decision-making, strategy, negotiation, and interpersonal dynamics for more than two dozen Fortune 500 companies. She has also held positions in systems engineering, equity derivatives, investment banking, and technology marketing. Her research, teaching, and consulting focus on how to turn around negative situations, with emphasis on improving both negotiation and decision-making, as well as interpersonal interactions. She holds a PhD in organizational behavior with a minor in psychology from Stanford University, a Master's degree in engineering-economic systems and an MBA from Stanford and a Bachelor's degree in systems engineering from the University of Virginia.

Dr Kahwajy's articles have appeared in *Harvard Business Review* ('How Management Teams Can Have a Good Fight,' July/August 1997), the *California Management Review* ('Conflict and Strategic Choice: How Top Management Teams Disagree,' Winter 1997), and in several books on entrepreneurship, change management, and strategic decision-making. She has been a Fellow with the Stanford Center on Conflict and Negotiation and is a member of the Academy of Management and the Institute for Operations Research and Management Sciences.

George Kohlrieser

George Kohlrieser, a clinical and organizational psychologist, is Professor of Organizational Behavior at IMD and consultant to global organizations around the world. In addition, he is Associate Clinical Professor of Psychology, Wright State University, Dayton, Ohio, and an adjunct faculty member of Union Graduate School, Antioch, Ohio, of Fielding Institute San Francisco, California, and of Zagreb University, Croatia. He specializes in conflict management, leadership, high-performance teamwork, change management, post-traumatic stress, and personal and professional development. He is also a police psychologist focusing on violence and aggression management, and hostage negotiations. He obtained his PhD from Ohio State University.

Professor Kohlrieser is the founder and director of Shiloah International, a consultancy offering integrated psychological services to profit and non-profit organizations. Shiloah International is the base for training in 50 countries in North and South America, Eastern and Western Europe, Africa, Australia and New Zealand, Asia, Russia, and India. He is president of the International Transactional Analysis Association in San Francisco, a non-profit scientific organization established to investigate and promote the use of transactional analysis (TA) in psychotherapy, education, business, and other fields of human interaction.

Colleen Lief

Colleen Lief joined IMD in 2000 as a research associate working on change management, marketing, and corporate learning issues. Soon after, she became the lead researcher at the IMD-Lombard Odier Darier Hentsch Family Business Research Center, where her research interests include corporate culture and adaptation. Ms Lief earned an MPhil degree in monetary economics at the University of Glasgow, Scotland, and a BSc in business administration from Duquesne University, Pittsburgh. She also pursued postgraduate work in political economy at the University of Texas, Dallas.

Prior to coming to IMD, Ms Lief garnered over 15 years of experience in the financial services sector. Previous positions have centered on international banking, commercial lending, and credit management at SunTrust Banks, Washington, DC and PNC Bank, Pittsburgh. Along with co-authors (and contributors to this book), Daniel Denison and John Ward, she published an article exploring the link between family business culture and performance, entitled 'Culture in Family-Owned Enterprises: Recognizing and Leveraging Unique Strengths' in the March 2004 edition of *Family Business Review*.

Peter Lorange

Dr Peter Lorange has been the President of IMD since July 1, 1993. He is Professor of Strategy and holds the Nestlé Chair. He is also co-director of two programs targeted at senior executives: Orchestrating Winning Performance and the Booster Program. He was formerly President of the Norwegian School of Management in Oslo. His areas of special interest are global strategic management, strategic planning, strategic alliances, and strategic control. He did his undergraduate studies at the Norwegian School of Economics and Business, was awarded an MA in operations management from Yale University, and a Doctor of Business Administration from Harvard University.

In management education, Dr Lorange was affiliated with the Wharton School, University of Pennsylvania, for more than a decade. He has also taught at the Sloan School of Management (MIT), IMEDE (now IMD), and the Stockholm School of Economics, at the undergraduate, master and doctoral levels. He has worked extensively within his areas of expertise with US, European, and Asian corporations, both in a consulting capacity and in executive education.

Dr Lorange has written or edited 16 books and over 130 articles. He serves on the board of several corporations, including S. Ugelstad Shipowners – his family business. He is also on the board of the Copenhagen Business School.

Joachim Schwass

Joachim Schwass is Professor of Family Business at IMD. He is co-director of the IMD-Lombard Odier Darier Hentsch Family Business Research Center and of IMD's renowned Leading the Family Business program. He also directs the annual IMD-Lombard Odier Darier Hentsch Distinguished Family Business Award. His main teaching focus is on owner-related management issues. He was educated in Germany, France, and Switzerland. He has attended graduate studies at Technische Universität Berlin and Université de Fribourg where he obtained a Lic.Rer.Pol. and a Dr.Rer.Pol.

Prior to joining IMD in 1992, he was managing director of several companies that were part of his own family's business. He managed industrial manufacturing businesses in Australia and the USA, as well as an international trading business in Switzerland. He has also started several international businesses. He is a board member of several international companies and of the Family Business Network (FBN) International, Lausanne.

Ulrich Steger

Ulrich Steger holds the Alcan Chair of Environmental Management at IMD and is director of IMD's research project on Corporate Sustainability Management (CSM). He is director of the DaimlerChrysler Partnership

Program and Allianz Excellence Program, as well as co-director of the Building High Performance Boards program. He holds a PhD from Ruhr University, Bochum.

Previously, Professor Steger was a full professor at the European Business School, a guest professor at St. Gallen University and a Fellow at Harvard University. Before becoming involved in management education, he was a member of the German Bundestag – specializing in energy, technology, industry, and foreign trade issues – and then Minister of Economics and Technology in the State of Hesse, with particular responsibility for transport, traffic, and energy.

Professor Steger is the author or editor of numerous publications, including *Mastering Global Corporate Governance*, *Managing Complex Mergers*, *Sustainable Development and Innovation in the Energy Sector*, *Corporate Diplomacy*, and *The Strategic Dimension of Environmental Management* (also available in Japanese, German, and Chinese). He is a member of the supervisory and advisory boards of several major companies and organizations; he was also a member of the managing board of Volkswagen, with responsibility for implementing an environmental strategy for VW worldwide.

John L. Ward
John Ward is The Wild Group Professor of Family Business at IMD, and also a professor at the Kellogg School of Management (USA). He is co-director of IMD's renowned Leading the Family Business program, in which he has taught since its inception in 1987. He is also co-director of the IMD-Lombard Odier Darier Hentsch Family Business Research Center. His teaching and research interests are in family enterprise continuity, governance, philanthropy, and sustainable strategy. His MBA and PhD degrees are from Stanford Graduate School of Business.

Professor Ward has authored several books, including the best-selling *Keeping the Family Business Healthy, Creating Effective Boards for Private Enterprises, Strategic Planning for the Family Business*, and the just published *Perpetuating the Family Business*, as well as the Family Business Leadership Series, several cases, and numerous articles. He serves on the board of four companies in Europe and North America.

IMD

IMD is one of the world's leading business schools. Located in Lausanne, Switzerland, IMD has been helping organizations improve their performance for over 50 years. Its high standards are recognized by hundreds of the best companies around the world.

IMD was founded by a group of leading corporations to address the real challenges that international business executives face and, in the final analysis, need to win. To this day, IMD remains focused on real-world management issues – developing leadership capabilities and offering state-of-the-art concepts and tools. While other business schools primarily teach full-time graduate university students, IMD keeps an unwavering focus on the learning needs of executives and their organizations.

Executive Development from IMD

Executive Development from IMD provides cutting-edge thinking from the faculty of one of the world's leading business schools.

Each book presents concepts and insights for today's most important business and management challenges. The tone is straightforward. The message is practical. The ideas are tested and ready for managers to apply in their companies.

Each book follows a similar format: key-point summaries reinforce the message of each chapter and learning points translate concepts into action. Every chapter is illustrated with relevant international case studies that bring the discussions, analysis, and recommendations to life.

Executives attend IMD programs not only to learn but also to be inspired. The books in this series, like IMD programs, provide executives with inspiration as well as with tools to improve themselves and make an immediate contribution to their companies. The focus is executive learning – engaging, energizing, and effective.

Preface

Perhaps in earlier times, managing the family business was much simpler. Families rallied behind their business for personal survival. Successors took up the family craft or trade without other choices. Family units remained intact till death. Lessons for business-owning families came from religions and philosophic stories on how family members should treat one another. The laws of life – and family business management – were clear, unambiguous.

Then, many businesses grew in scale and scope and the family owners had to depend on other employees and managers. Family norms changed in many parts of the world. Society presented new, diverse opportunities to competent heirs. Market capitalization made business assets that could be bought and sold.

A conventional wisdom emerged: family ownership resulted in inferior businesses. Nepotism was bad, unjust. Family dynamics tore apart businesses. Families clung to the stability and security of past practices in a rapidly changing world. Business schools called for the 'professionalism' of management – meaning the separation of ownership and control. Maximizing shareholder value became the gospel for sophisticated companies. Families in business were counseled to separate their family from their businesses, and 'manage your business like a business; your family like a family' became the credo.

This advice, this wisdom, recognized the fundamental challenge for family businesses: how to cope with the frictions between family needs and business requirements as illustrated in Figure 1.

The message was simple. Separate them as much as possible. And where not possible, define the boundaries precisely and in favor of the business. After all, if the family wrecks the company, what is left? Don't kill the goose that lays the golden eggs.

IMD's faculty has been close to hundreds of the leading family businesses in the world for nearly 20 years. That experience provides the insight that many of the most successful families in business do not see life as being so simple and do not accept the mantra of separating the family from the business. Instead, they see family ownership as a special advantage to the business. And they find special opportunities for the family as owners of the business.

Rather than seeing the relationships between the family and the business as a dilemma requiring artful compromise between the two, they see a synthesis between family ownership and business success.

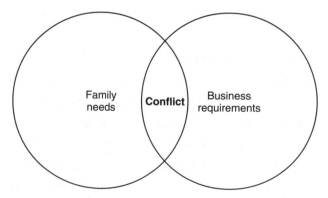

Figure 1   Family and/or business

Early research suggested family-controlled firms were not inferior forms of enterprise. In fact, they performed better (Ward, 1983). Recently many studies have further documented the competitive advantage and superior performance of family-controlled companies (see for example Anderson and Reeb, 2003). Family firms also compete and behave differently from non-family firms, as will be portrayed in this book.

Understanding that families and the businesses they run are not only a source of mutual conflict, but also a source of mutual benefit requires paradoxical thinking. How can these contradictions both be true? How do enterprising families mold family and business together successfully? How do families overcome the added stress of business ownership? These are the questions addressed in this book.

The answers lie in innovative thinking about businesses and about families. Family businesses diverge in fundamental ways from the conventional wisdoms of management teaching. Consider, for example, the contrasts in Table 1. While certainly not all businesses fit neatly into one column or the other, the differences are thought-provoking.

To appreciate the unconventional wisdoms followed by successful families in business requires counterintuitive insight. IMD's approach to executive education encourages counterintuitive thinking. Faculty members are coached to listen first; participants come from many diverse backgrounds; everyone is emotionally engaged; class sessions seek synthesis of competing ideas.

What successful families in business do best is to proactively accept that contradictions can coexist. There are contradictions in many critical dimensions. See Figure 2. These dimensions are the topics of this book.

To see the depths and resolutions to these contradictions requires a broader conceptual model of family business. Beyond noting the interaction of

Table 1 Family businesses are different

For the family firm	For the non-family firm
The purpose is continuity	The purpose is maximizing near-term share price
The goal is to preserve the assets and reputation of the owning family	The goal is to meet institutional investor expectations
The fundamental belief is that the first priority is to protect downside risk	The fundamental belief is that more risk promises return
The strategic orientation is adaptation	The strategic orientation is constant growth
The management focus is continuous incremental improvement	The management focus is innovation
The most important stakeholders are customers and employees	The most important stakeholders are shareholders and management
The business is seen as a social institution	The business is seen as a disposable asset
Leadership is stewardship	Leadership is personal charisma

family with business, shown earlier in Figure 1, it is helpful to capture the confounding dimensions of ownership and individuality as well, shown in Figure 3. The concentrated ownership of a family-controlled firm hugely affects strategy, culture, succession, and governance. Ownership is also a source of collective pride and disparate goals within the family.

Bonding the family together as a harmonious team is culturally important for ownership effectiveness and business clarity. Yet, doing so, without simultaneously appreciating individual differences and the need for freedom is destined to fail. Ownership is both a group concept and also a personal privilege and responsibility.

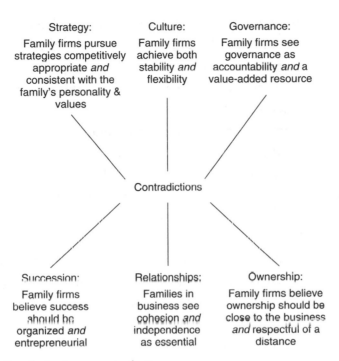

Strategy:
Family firms pursue strategies competitively appropriate *and* consistent with the family's personality & values

Culture:
Family firms achieve both stability *and* flexibility

Governance:
Family firms see governance as accountability *and* a value-added resource

Contradictions

Succession:
Family firms believe success should be organized *and* entrepreneurial

Relationships:
Families in business see cohesion *and* independence as essential

Ownership:
Family firms believe ownership should be close to the business *and* respectful of a distance

Figure 2   Family business contradictions

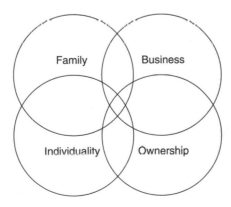

Family   Business

Individuality   Ownership

Figure 3   Conceptual model of family business

In sum, because family-controlled businesses are different they require a different set of insights. Blending family and business raises many contradictions. Successful business-owning families reconcile these differences and contradictions with counterintuitive thinking and unconventional actions. This book shows these lessons as discovered by IMD's family business teaching and research team.

Chapter 1 by IMD's President, Peter Lorange, describes the particular dilemmas facing family firms in pursuit of the growth imperative. He proposes that it is actually through focusing on promoting an atmosphere of openness and individual entrepreneurial development that these challenges are conquered.

Chapter 2 explains that the superior profitability of successful family firms is directly related to the degree to which they embrace unconventional strategies. The characteristically inimitable strategies of family firms organically create special competitive advantages. Counterintuitively, nepotism and constrained financial resources can be advantages in themselves.

Chapter 3 calls for the integration of family strategic planning with business strategic planning. Doing so is not an inappropriate inconvenience, but a necessity and a source of business strength. Family values and vision shape company strategy at least as much as market analysis.

In Chapter 4 Colleen Lief, research director of IMD's Lombard Odier Darier Hentsch Family Business Research Center, teams with Professor Daniel Denison to present new research on the surprising distinctiveness of family business culture. Drawing upon Professor Denison's unique database, they find that family firms maintain a culture that is both internally *and* externally focused and results in both stability *and* flexibility.

Chapters 5 and 6 examine the most obvious of family business challenges – succession. All surveys point to succession as the most difficult issue. Professor Joachim Schwass, long-time co-director of IMD's Leading the Family Business program, has studied succession in many successful and globally recognized firms. He sees the successor as the prime actor in succession, not as the passive participant, or victim. He presents a new multiphase process that can enhance succession. He offers personal, professional, and business growth as the core of succession planning.

Chapters 7 and 8 look at family relationships in fresh ways. First, Professor George Kohlrieser, as a result of his intense hostage negotiating experiences, encourages a different, more powerful, way to view conflict resolution in families. He challenges them to confront their conflict avoidance tendencies. He argues that it is essential to address personal needs before interests and to create stronger bonds, even when they are assumed to be a given. He further contradicts conventional thinking when he states that concession-making is not a weakness in negotiations. Professor and psychologist Jean L. Kahwajy then takes the subject of family conflict further. She believes that conflict is good in families and that, in fact, meaningful communication actually creates, requires conflict. If individuals did not disagree, they would have no need to communicate and would miss the closeness that can result.

Professor Kahwajy puts the focus for effective communication on the individual, as Professor Schwass does for succession. The receiver of communication affects the ultimate outcome more than the sender and plays a key role in healthy interaction.

Chapter 9 offers new research on another critical subject for business families: the family constitution. The family constitution is perhaps one of the three most widely recommended prescriptions to families in business. (The others are communications, as explored in the previous two chapters, and governance, which will be discussed in the following two chapters.) Yet there has been virtually no research on the nature and effectiveness of family constitutions. This chapter looks most closely at the process – not the content – of drafting the family constitution as the key to success. The common presumption of who is best qualified to lead the process is also questioned.

In Chapter 10 Professor Ulrich Steger applies decades of work leading the study of governance to the subject of the family business board. Though family firms are often exempt from new governance regulations, Professor Steger sees that both as good news and bad. He challenges the whole notion of the impact of governance rules and proposes that success boils down to a question of 'fit.' And, family-controlled firms have the special opportunity and responsibility to assert their core values and principles as the most vital instrument of governance.

Chapter 11 looks at the role of family owners in the governance process. As discussed at the beginning of this Preface, conventional wisdom holds that family and business should be kept separate. Nowhere is this concept more contentious than in the consideration of the line between family owners and the company's board and management. Yet successful families in business see great value in close relationships between the owners and the managers, as well as active involvement on the board.

Chapter 12 attempts to summarize the counterintuitive insights and unconventional strategies discussed throughout the book. For family firms, strategy, culture, succession, and governance are different, as are the special challenges of effective family communications and conflict management. Harnessing all these differences is what makes the family-controlled company not the less-than-optimal organizational form believed by many, but, perhaps an enterprise with a special 'DNA' for distinct competitive advantage.

References

Anderson, R.C. and Reeb, D.M. 2003. 'Founding-family ownership and firm performance: evidence from the S&P 500' *Journal of Finance*, Vol. 58, Iss. 3.

Ward, J.L. 1983. 'The impact of family business on marketing strategy and performance,' in Hills, G. (ed.), *Marketing and Entrepreneurship*. Washington, DC: American Marketing Association.

Acknowledgments

Assembling and contributing to this book has been an exciting and stimulating experience. Collaborating with faculty colleagues of such international respect in their personal subjects of interest and exploring with them the unique theses of this book has been a privilege. Their care for families in business and their creativity in relating to family enterprises has brought great benefit to the field and to the school over the past years.

IMD's President, Peter Lorange, inspired this book. His genuine personal support for, and interest in, family business has made learning about family firms and teaching families in business a cherished part of IMD.

Colleen Lief made the book possible. As a researcher she has contributed great value to the topics. As a writer she sets the example for us all. As book project manager she has been a gifted professional. Steve Waichler, Inna Francis, Patricia Butler, Anita Slomski, and Michelle Perrinjaquet also contributed immeasurably. Their support and their editing skills were essential, and greatly appreciated.

The ideas and the spirit of this book came from the families who have studied at IMD. They shared, they challenged, they provided purpose. To them, and to other families in business, the message of the book is simply: Appreciate your differences, trust your experienced intuitions, pursue your distinctiveness; dare to be unconventional.

And, finally, take hope – for virtually every difficult challenge presented in this book, the power to achieve and to succeed often rests with the individual. Each person has the power to shape and direct the entire family's effectiveness. The individual successor can take responsibility for succession. The individual owner can contribute with competence. Individual family managers can lead the business's culture. Family leadership is a constellation of many individual leaders. 'Family Business' is not an oxymoron. The role of the individual resolves the seeming paradox. Blending family and business is rarely a compromise to both. Rather the successful find it as a synthesis, drawing on the respect for the individual and bonded by shared family values.

John L. Ward
Wild Group Professor of Family Business
Co-Director, Lombard Odier Darier Hentsch
Family Business Research Center
IMD
Lausanne, Switzerland

1
The Growth Dilemma in Family-Owned Firms

Peter Lorange

IMD – International Institute for Management Development – has been the global meeting place for families in business since 1988. For almost two decades members of more than 600 families from more than 60 countries have been coming to IMD's campus in Lausanne for family business education. Most have participated in the renowned Leading the Family Business program; many other family business leaders have taken part in collaborative programs with the Family Business Network, with industry groups, and with IMD's Building High Performance Boards program.

Confronting this global diversity challenges IMD faculty to think wider and deeper and differently. Conventional paradigms of thought are tested as top executives from the world's most sophisticated businesses share their experiences and views. Learning at IMD is a two-way street. The faculty learn from successful family firms; families in business learn from the real-world research of the faculty. Conventional wisdom comes face to face with reality. New ideas and new insights are inevitable. Many are counterintuitive, at first. The real world is always more complex than current theory.

IMD prides itself on its constant quest for fresh and different thinking. It is able to facilitate this search as a result of its global perspective and its constant interaction – in the classroom and outside – with leading business leaders and owners. IMD is devoted to *developing* new practical knowledge, not just teaching it.

Nowhere is this philosophy more important than in family firms. There has been remarkably little research into family-controlled businesses, yet, with their very special challenges, they are in many ways a distinct type of business from which all organizations can learn. IMD is committed to providing the leadership to unlock these mysteries. IMD's Lombard Odier Darier Hentsch Family Business Research Center is devoted to developing ground-breaking research for the leading family businesses of the world.

While many things are different about family firms, compared with other companies, one thing is not: the imperative to grow the company. All too often family firms fail to appreciate that company growth helps fuel everything else; all too often they let their culture and family priorities block their ability to grow. But in the end, the issue is 'either you grow or you eventually go out of business.' There are, however, two particularly thorny issues when it comes to growth in family-owned firms. One has to do with the 'silos,' or 'kingdoms,' that can form within family firms as a result of their very nature. For example, certain family members with executive positions in the firm might feel that they have 'territorial rights' to some parts of the firm and do not necessarily see the need to communicate more broadly, in a more 'meeting place oriented' atmosphere. Whereas professional managers tend to realize that they must perform or be forced to leave, their family-business counterparts might see their jobs as absolutely secure.

A second issue that affects growth in family-owned firms has to do with developing 'internal entrepreneurs' so that they can function properly.

Here, the family-members-cum-owners often feel that they need to have total control over growth initiatives. They simply do not want to allow outsiders in to play the internal entrepreneur role. On the other side of the coin, professional managers might feel that younger family members will eventually be given such opportunities, so the motivation for taking on difficult, energy-consuming internal entrepreneur roles might be limited. It will therefore typically be hard to attract outsiders for such critical assignments.

A disguised case study will illustrate these issues. The two above-mentioned challenges are of course found in *all* corporations, not only in family-controlled firms. But, as we shall argue, they can often be particularly difficult to cope with in such a setting.

Case study

Company X is a third-generation family-owned firm, with the family holding all of the shares in the company. Not surprisingly, the CEO is a family member. He has two sons and a son-in-law actively involved in the business. There are three divisions, one of which is run by one of the sons. The other two divisions are run by outside professionals. The other son is the chief strategic officer, a staff position. The son-in-law is presently a special projects manager, working on ad hoc business development issues.

The company employs more than a thousand people and has been growing at a strong rate, with a compound average of 10% per year sales growth over the last five years. The profitability of the company has also been strong. Moderate dividends have been paid out to the family members, but the board, consisting entirely of family members, has reaffirmed the long-term objectives of the firm, namely to be willing to invest for future growth, and therefore to pay only relatively moderate dividends. Realistic growth is therefore *the* key agenda item.

Recently, however, the company has faced two difficult issues relating to growth, as follows.

Silos, kingdoms

As noted, one of the sons heads one division; outside professional executives head the other two divisions. Over time, a culture has developed in which each division sees itself as entirely freestanding. Know-how, technologies and clients have come to be viewed as divisional property, not as corporate-owned assets. Could this perhaps eventually limit the firm's growth prospects? Indeed, the CEO had belatedly reached this conclusion – but how could the firm crack this silo mentality?

Specifically, how could a 'meeting place' culture be developed between the divisions so that opportunities could be examined in a broader context? For example, if the strengths of the various divisions were considered together, this might reveal new strategic opportunities for the whole firm. Thus, perhaps clients that have traditionally been served by one division could be addressed on a broader, company-wide basis. Furthermore, by combining the intellectual efforts of the entire management team, not only drawing on the know-how of the subteams in each division, specific challenges could perhaps be handled more effectively.

The problem, however, seems to be that each division has become too accustomed to being on its own and its attitudes are quite entrenched.

In particular, the behavior of the son who is division president seems to promote this. He feels that it is essential for him to have a degree of independence – a certain mandate – relative to his father, whom he sees as rather dominant. Also, he feels that his position gives him a right to independence, more generally, compared with the rest of the family. His way of coping is to say, 'Leave me alone to run my division and don't interfere with me.' While the CEO/father clearly appreciates this to some extent, it also seems to be the case that the dynamics of the father–son relationship – or more broadly the relationship between any family members working together – often leads the 'junior' party to feel the need to retain independence. Family-specific arguments can, however, be taken too far – even to the extent of being used as an 'excuse' for having silos! After all, companies are meant to be communities of executives working together, so using a family relationship and the need for sibling independence as an 'argument' against a broader 'meeting place' cooperation might be seen as dysfunctional.

With the division run by one of the sons taking such an independent stance, it is easy to see why the other divisions have developed similar behavior. They are also using the precedents set by the family-member-led division as the basis for developing wider independence and autonomy. The net effect has been that Company X has not been able to create a 'meeting place' culture, where opportunities are pursued on a broader basis, where potential challenges or even problems are resolved based on the maximum capabilities of the group, and where technical and commercial assets are in effect seen as 'suboptimal' when they relate to a particular division only. Clearly, the ability to pursue effective growth is at stake here. An inbuilt tendency for family-owned firms to develop a particularly strong silo mentality can indeed result in growth being compromised.

The internal entrepreneur dilemma

Internal entrepreneurs are typically needed to help spearhead internally generated growth. Such internal entrepreneurs need to have *both* an ability to see business opportunities before they are obvious to everyone else, i.e., a clear commercial sense, *and* an ability to know where the internal resources are in the firm and to be able to draw on all of them – as well as on resources from outside if they are not available internally. They must be able to inspire and lead typically 'flat,' new business development teams, relying on their own innovative leadership capabilities, rather than on a hierarchical sense of power and control. The internal entrepreneur clearly needs to be close to the CEO, who can provide the necessary backing and support for the usual requests for additional resources, as well as recognizing the need to take certain risks. The CEO can also offer 'cover' when critical voices are raised, as so often happens with growth projects. Perhaps paradoxically, the internal entrepreneur also needs a certain distance from the CEO, i.e., the freedom to maneuver, to move fast, without the constraints of micro-management and having to ask for permission to do everything.

What, then, are the problems when it comes to developing internal entrepreneurs in the family firm? And why is the ideal profile for an internal entrepreneur in the family-owned firm so hard to develop? In the case of Company X, for example, should the CEO/father appoint his son who is the chief strategic officer to spearhead internal entrepreneurship, or should he ask his son-in-law to do it as part of his ad hoc business development? Or should he ignore the family and choose an outsider for the role?

First, when it comes to seeing business opportunities, family members may not always find it easy to 'tolerate' the idea of an outsider having a more insightful approach to the business. All too often, the situation arises because family members feel that they 'know best' what a good business approach is – and that they need to know best because of their position. They might find it difficult to allow others to come up with 'more insightful' ideas. Clearly, on the one hand, it might be hard for an internal entrepreneur from the outside to compete with the family and, on the other hand, an internal entrepreneur from the family itself might be too shortsighted in his or her views on new breakthrough business opportunities.

Second, identifying *where* the resources can be mobilized *from* can also be a difficult task in the family firm. Family members often have particular favorites – sympathies and antipathies – in terms of both business areas and employees. Thus some parts of the firm might be called on heavily for business ideas and support, while other parts might be ignored through lack of understanding of what they can offer. Similarly, when it comes to outside resources, some family members might have particular views on *which* outside entities to work with, often based on other motives, such as previous family history, past conflicts or friction. The net result is that in a family firm it might be more difficult to mobilize the optimal mix of resources needed to go after a new growth opportunity. If a family member is the internal entrepreneur, he or she might have a rather shortsighted, even blinkered, view of where the relevant resources might be. Conversely, if the internal entrepreneur is a non-family member, there might be too many 'sacred cows' that he or she cannot mobilize.

Third, when it comes to inspirational leadership, which is so critical in growth-oriented, project-based 'flat' team initiatives, it can perhaps be more difficult for a family member to play the role of an effective catalyst. The perception might be that he or she has the mandate by inheritance. Whether the family member in question is competent or not can often be difficult to 'prove,' since the rest of the organization typically assumes – often justifiably – that he or she attained the position through the family connection and did not necessarily earn it by performing well. Hence, it is often difficult for a family-member-cum-internal-entrepreneur to effectively lead a growth team. But the dilemma in deciding who to appoint is that a non-family internal entrepreneur might find it equally difficult to lead the growth team, given that he or she will have to rely on family members for legitimacy and the power to perform the leadership tasks in question. And, above all, how can he or she have a deeper business insight than the family members who have grown up in the business?

Fourth, as noted, the CEO should in theory give the internal entrepreneur 'cover,' so that resources can be allocated to the growth project on a strategic basis to achieve a breakthrough dimension – *not* merely incremental extensions of the present situation – and so that the inevitable risks can be taken. In practice, it is often hard for a family firm with a family CEO to allow a non-family member to enjoy this independence and accord him or her the necessary support. The family CEO may want to reserve these types of powers for him- or herself and/or for close family, say, offspring. By contrast, in the case of a family member who is the internal entrepreneur, the issue might be that the CEO family member cannot be seen to be favoring one of his family over the others. The family CEO may therefore be reluctant to provide special support to one family member and not to the others. Once again, the result might be a weakened internal entrepreneur function.

Finally, when it comes to the 'distance' between the CEO and the internal entrepreneur, the arguments follow similar lines. A non-family internal entrepreneur might not be given sufficient freedom and distance because the CEO and/or other family members may, deep down, resent having someone outside the clan running new business initiatives. If, on the other hand, it is a family member who is the internal entrepreneur, the CEO might find it equally difficult to grant him or her the necessary freedom, at the expense of the others.

Overall, establishing an effective platform for internal entrepreneurs in a family firm can be difficult. Whether the internal entrepreneur is a family member or not, there are deep dilemmas.

Any solutions?

It is, of course, difficult to come up with simple solutions to these dilemmas. Perhaps one of the most important factors to recognize is that internally generated growth depends fundamentally on a number of organizational culture issues – and these need to be addressed whether it is a family firm or not. Specifically, a growth culture needs to encompass:

- A 'meeting place' cultural dimension, where opportunities are discussed on a wider basis, say, once a month for a day or so, and typically with a rather open-ended agenda. These 'retreats' should be as free-flowing as possible, with no hasty decisions taken or quick conclusions drawn; they should simply be a brainstorming forum. Perhaps through this sort of experience, one might see the benefits of such a 'meeting place' culture when it comes to creating more powerful ideas for growth.
- A 'must do' cultural dimension is also key. In family firms, the concern that everyone has for each other might typically lead to slow decision-making. People do not want to hurt each other's feelings. Again, an open, brainstorming 'meeting place' approach might lead to more of a 'must do' culture.

- A clear business plan pointing toward growth is also necessary, where one builds on established strengths, either by taking these strengths into new markets and/or by selectively adding new competences to broaden the business base, by carefully adding to the strengths. Here, experience has clearly shown: internal entrepreneurs are typically *critical* for spearheading these growth initiatives based on one's strength. Again, the realization that business growth is not magic, but simply depends on using the positions one has already established, might serve to depoliticize the image of the internal entrepreneur, might make the internal entrepreneur more legitimate. Perhaps this can help to develop a climate of acceptance of internal entrepreneurs in family firms, to establish a more realistic basis for growth.

Conclusion

Family firms often respond well to the growth challenge, and their performance reflects this. There is no doubt that they can have many advantages – particularly relative to large publicly traded firms, which are often overly complex and political. The challenge for the family-owned firm is to make sure that politics stemming from family dynamics are minimized and that bureaucracy is not allowed to develop based on family considerations. The following chapters of this book raise particular dilemmas for family firms and show the unconventional approaches successful family firms around the globe have used. In these chapters, IMD faculty members share their counterintuitive thinking as they tackle the real-world issues of enterprising families.

References for further reading

Chakravarthy, B. and Lorange, P. 2005. 'Nurturing corporate entrepreneurship,' in Strebel, P. (ed.), *Executive Learning: Where Content Meets Context and Emotion*. London: Pearson.

Herbold, R.J. 2004. *The Fiefdom Syndrome*. New York: Doubleday.

2
Unconventional Strategy: Why Family Firms Outperform

John L. Ward

The superior performance of family firms runs counter to conventional wisdom. The most common perception of families in business is found in the expression: 'Shirt Sleeves to Shirt Sleeves.' This concept of a three-generation cycle of rags-to-riches-to-rags is found in many languages and cultures. The idea is so universal that it is hard to dismiss. In fact, if we take a close look at family businesses, we can find many common problems that would explain the old adage. Families grow and change with each generational succession and often their businesses do, too. Both families and businesses tend to change scale exponentially, making their effective union increasingly complex over time. Balancing the demands of growing families and businesses is a challenge that compounds with each generation, and this makes sustaining their mutual success ever more difficult.

Stories of family failure are quite common, and known to all. The deleterious effects of nepotism are one example of such received wisdom. Everyone knows the story of the boss's son, who is unqualified but still chosen to lead, and ends up destroying the company. Another common tale is found in the 'feuding relatives,' who are often fighting about money, or whose offspring is next CEO, and running the business into the ground. In fact, every family in business must overcome conflicts within both the family and the company, and often simultaneously. This combination causes the mixing of inter-personal family dynamics with the strategic needs and direction of the business, and would seem to explain the common notion of family business failure.

A careful examination of these family business dynamics provides more reasons to support conventional wisdom, than to refute it. In case after case, family problems and conflict are superimposed on their businesses. Nepotism is a real issue and can lead to adverse leadership selection and distorted compensation. Succession and remuneration are a common source of conflict in many families. Indeed, many business decisions can trigger family conflict, and maintaining a healthy family business system necessarily involves balancing business and family issues and managing conflict. At times, holding the family together can become more difficult than resolving strategic business issues, and there are many examples of family dynamics driving business decisions.

Conventional wisdom frowns on this, believing that rational, business precepts should always guide decisions.

The other common negative idea is that family owners are in competition with their business for capital. Ownership is seen as favoring the extraction of capital, rather than supporting needed business investments. Generation successions can trigger estate taxes, too, creating external demands on capital. Many family companies remain privately held, limiting their access to outside investors, and potentially creating a shortage of capital when strategic investment is needed. Private family firms can be squeezed between growing shareholder demands for distributions or liquidity, and business challenges or opportunities that demand fundamental redeployment of capital.

The closer one looks at family business dynamics, the more reasons there are to believe conventional wisdom, and yet research increasingly shows that family businesses have, on average, both higher financial performance and greater long-term continuity. How can this be?

Understanding this dichotomy will require new and counterintuitive thinking. Figuring out family business success requires a change of mindset and digging below the surface. IMD has the oldest and most popular family-business executive education course in the world. Through the years the executives of family firms have provided many new insights into this puzzle. Quite a few of these executives come from family businesses that are very successful and long-lived. In fact, about 15% of the 600 families who have taken IMD's course are over 100 years old. A close look at their business strategies reveals many creative, distinct, and cleverly designed approaches to business. In fact, their unusual and unpredictable strategic disparity is likely their unifying element. These strategies display a high degree of adaptation and specificity that at first glance defies explanation.

This experience at IMD has generated the fundamental conclusion that *family firms and the families that own them succeed by pursuing unconventional strategies and thinking*. The more that is learned, the more need there is to dismiss negative assumptions and dispense with conventional wisdom, if the success of family businesses is to be penetrated and understood. Instead of assuming family dynamics are problematic and strategies irrational, it would be better to look at them positively and seek a change of mindset. How can these characteristics of family businesses be seen as positive rather than negative, as value-creating rather than value-destroying? Data from research increasingly suggests that conventional wisdom is wrong. To really understand family business success will require thinking in counterintuitive ways. This lesson seems particularly clear in relation to understanding business strategy in family firms.

Turning negatives to positives in nepotism

The first and most fundamental set of negative assumptions about family businesses relates to the role of family ownership. The distinct, concentrated ownership groups of family companies are one of their most distinguishing characteristics. Rather than assuming family ownership is a drain and a liability for the family firm, this particular form of ownership might be understood as an asset to the business. It is clear that the concentrated ownership of family firms can facilitate control of the business. Smaller ownership groups, coupled with good governance, can more directly control their enterprises and achieve greater agility. By facilitating a close alignment of ownership and business interests and strategy, family businesses can leverage competitive advantages – even unconventional ones – that other businesses cannot.

Conventional wisdom views family involvement in management as potentially hazardous. The issues created by nepotism are real, but the direct involvement of owners in management and governance can be viewed positively as well. This close involvement enables the concentrated control characteristic of family businesses, and helps assure that ownership and business interests are directly linked and mutually informed. This direct, long-term connection enables challenging short-term decision-making, and reinforces a shared long-term vision and alignment of strategic goals. Family businesses often feature close, personal relationships between owners and business leaders (even non-family executives), which can enable a higher degree of mutual trust and understanding. This, in turn, can enable greater business agility in both problem-solving and strategy selection. The high degree of alignment between business interests and the concentrated control of family ownership can be a powerful facilitator for unusual strategic adaptations, which can enable competitive advantage and lead to higher rates of success.

On close examination, family managers have more to offer than close ties to ownership. While nepotism can create serious weaknesses in management, more often family successors add value in unique ways. They have been 'schooled' in the family business since early youth, collecting the 'idiosyncratic knowledge' embedded in family managers over generations. Family managers often know what it takes for their businesses to be successful. They know the history of industry cycles, take a long-term view of business development, and understand the importance of different stakeholders to the company. They are known to customers and suppliers since youth. They also place a high value on the company's reputation, and bring a deep understanding of the company's values, principles and culture. These lessons are learned over the generations, and the transmission of this 'idiosyncratic knowledge' from generation to generation is a key value-added of family management successors.

In addition, family successors often have a very special passion for the business. They place a high personal value on the close reflection of culture and values shared between the business and the family. Often, family leaders have their name on the door, and the reputations and identity of the business and the family are mutually defined. In times of change, family successors are more attentive to issues of cultural continuity, which often leads them to pursue more creative and adaptive business solutions. This reflects a common preference for values-based, long-term solutions that can both preserve and enhance capital creation.

Family successors also tend to have a different approach to business risk. They rarely take the larger fashionable or speculative risks that more egocentric, short-term motivated executives would take in a non-family business. Instead, they tend to take a long-term approach, often focusing first on business continuity and preserving value. They can be risk-takers, too, but their approach to driving business growth is often guided by a desire to create and transmit the greatest value to future generations. Instead of focusing on strategies that will create big short-term returns, they focus on what will create the most value over time. They are predisposed to pursuing business growth that is solid, dependable and sustainable, and they can also take risks that have their highest potential payoff far in the future. Family business leaders tend to focus on building value in the business for the next generation. This generational perspective of value creation may be the single, largest intangible asset family successors bring to business leadership.

None of these qualities are understood or valued by conventional wisdom. Instead, according to convention, the most important characteristics to assess in choosing business leaders are their professional qualifications and experience. Candidates for the most senior management positions are expected to be supremely competent and to have demonstrated a history of success in a long climb up the management ladder. Family successors are often chosen based on their qualities of character and judgment, rather than long tenures of experience while working their way up through management. Some family managers have the ultimate 'fast track,' and they spend their early careers preparing to lead. Often, they are systematically exposed to different parts of the business, jumping from 'ladder to ladder' rather than staying on a single, narrow path to the top. This can give family leaders a breadth of knowledge about the company, and may enable them to see a bigger, less provincial picture of the business.

Most often, conventional wisdom views the 'fast track' of succession in family business as a liability, rather than an asset. It is nepotism at work – and conventional thinking does not find any of the 'idiosyncratic' value-added to be discovered in family successors. In addition, it does not value the special preparation and training of family successors, who often begin preparing for leadership very early in life. Many of them also benefit from a highly tailored and unusually systematic training for their future responsibilities. Family successors often aspire early on to leadership positions, which tends to increase their motivation and commitment during their preparation. All of these elements point out the potential value of a 'fast track' to leadership for family members.

But this stereotype of the 'fast track' also does not do justice to the complexity of succession in family business. A close look at family business cases reveals that many family managers have unusually long tenures in the business before becoming leaders. Succession in family businesses is often delayed by the long careers of family leaders, whose tenures can stretch out for many decades. Family successors often have a great deal of experience, and sometimes transition through periods of shared inter-generational leadership. Successful family companies have non-family leaders in top management. Family companies can and do recognize the importance of competencies and experience, and they are willing to look beyond family candidates, when appropriate. Leadership in many family firms tends to evolve toward more of a team approach over time, as the family grows into a collaboration of siblings and then cousins. This may make leadership systems more adaptive in family firms, allowing the strengths of both family and non-family managers to be better utilized.

The counterintuitive advantage of capital constraint

Many family companies remain privately held for generations. They often grow for long periods of time with little external capital, including debt. The debt aversion found among many family companies is unusual, and conventional wisdom would hold that it is wrong not to leverage access to this less expensive capital. The public equity market is another source of capital that is often ignored by family companies, even though equities can be sold while voting control is retained. As a result, many family companies are perceived as operating with 'artificially' limited capital resources. They could, in fact, have access to much more capital, if they were willing to fully leverage the value of their businesses, and this, in turn, would enable greater investment for strategic breadth and opportunities of scale. If nothing else, the self-imposed capital limitations of family businesses should make them slower-growing and give them a competitive disadvantage to other more flexible, aggressive and proactive firms.

The capital constraint in family businesses is often a hangover from the entrepreneurial stage of the business. At the entrepreneurial stage, most businesses operate under capital constraints. Lenders or investors are looking for a consistent track record of sales and profits, and raising external capital can be very expensive for a startup company. As a result, many young businesses must generate their own working capital internally, and plow profits back into the company for growth. Family business founders are often more focused on building capital and keeping it in the business, than on extracting profits – even late in life. This frugal culture of reinvestment is often established by a founder and passed down to succeeding generations. Many family businesses continue to rely on disciplined, internal capital generation long after their companies could have ready access to inexpensive debt. Also, family-controlled firms tend to pay out less in dividends by a large amount.

Conventional wisdom holds that these self-imposed capital constraints should put family businesses at a disadvantage. But their superior performance motivates counterintuitive thinking again, and the question: 'Could the discipline of operating with limited capital benefit family businesses?' A close look at many case studies shows that the discipline imposed by constrained capital is a great source of business focus and motivation. It tends to sharpen strategy and increase the creativity of strategy selection. There is also more at stake in the initial execution of a strategy and a greater motivation to achieve performance success quickly. The inherent frugality of the system also engenders continuous attention to making cost improvements and keeping corporate overheads down.

In addition, digging deeper into the question reveals that a lack of capital drives many family businesses to less capital-intensive strategies, which have lower risk and are often based on more intangible elements of value creation. Intangibles like reputation, quality, and brand recognition are all common examples of value-added elements found in many successful family businesses. In addition, family businesses seem more adept at successfully executing strategies that others find costly to administer and conventional wisdom frowns on. Vertical integration and diversification are two examples of disfavored strategies that family businesses seem better adapted to execute effectively and efficiently. The inherent frugality and concentrated control of family businesses gives them an unusual ability to control costs in the execution of many strategies.

The frugal nature of family businesses also manifests in another important way. Just as founding entrepreneurs seek to retain and build value in the business, succeeding generations are often also motivated to avoid value extraction. Every time value is extracted, taxation dilutes it. Dividends are taxed as income; redemptions or sales of stock are taxed as capital gains; and gift or estate taxes on ownership transfers can be so significant that they create a need to extract capital. Indeed, taxation can become such a drain on capital that it will either challenge the family's ability to retain control or the business's ability to reinvest. Yet, the family business can be a particularly effective vehicle for wealth creation and transfer because it aligns business and ownership interests for avoiding taxation and retaining capital in the business.

Limited liquidity is a counterintuitive benefit of the capital constraints found in many family businesses. Family owners are often captive investors, which keeps them both more engaged with their businesses and more focused on the issues of long-term value creation and transfer. Tax planning is an essential element of this focus, and the ability to align ownership and business interests in this process can be particularly powerful. Managing decisions to avoid or minimize taxes and preserve cash can benefit the family and the business in many ways. In privately held companies, valuation discounting can be applied in transfer taxes, and discounts for minority interests and lack of liquidity can greatly reduce the tax burden. In addition, transfer tax issues can cause families to pursue collective ownership vehicles to achieve further discounting or to shelter future growth from taxation. All of these strategies benefit the business by avoiding capital extraction for paying taxes, and they benefit the family by transferring a higher percentage of the wealth retained in the company.

Stories about families that sell or break up their businesses in order to achieve liquidity are very common, but rarely do we hear the other side. Capital constraints that limit liquidity often cause families to come together and work closely. They can engender collective ownership vehicles, shareholder agreements, and other innovative governance structures. In fact, capital constraints often serve to keep the interests of growing, and increasingly disparate, families closely aligned with the best interests of their businesses. Family owners recognize that many liquidity solutions trigger increased taxation for everyone and dilute ownership control. The mutual economic interests shared by many individual family owners in their business can provide a powerful motivation for maintaining the concentrated governance control that enables an effective ongoing alignment of business and ownership interests. This motivation is often powerfully reinforced by a culture of business frugality, and, in combination, these factors often lead to a strategic focus on future, long-term value creation and transfer, rather than liquidity.

Learning from vertical integration and diversification

Looking more closely at the problems of vertical integration and diversification can reveal more about the unusual strengths of family business. In vertical integration, a parent company owns different pieces of a single supply chain, so that different parts of the company are competing with one another for profits through pricing. In diversification, where the parent company owns businesses in a variety of unrelated industries, internal capital allocation – and reallocation – is often disputed, and little opportunity to leverage industry scale is achieved. In both strategies, the multiple strengths, weaknesses and needs of internally competing businesses must be weighed and balanced, and, according to conventional wisdom, this is an expensive process to govern and leads to larger corporate overheads. These strategies are also thought to lead inevitably to the underperformance of at least one of the businesses. Family businesses, however, with their combination of capital constraints and concentrated control, seem particularly well adapted to making these strategies work effectively.

Fundamentally, it is the frugality of family business systems that is the base of their vertical integration and diversification strategy success. Rather than address the administrative control of these complex strategies with lots of corporate overheads, family businesses depend on their culture to control the integration and efficiency. Vertical integration is often a cost-control strategy related to the supply chain, where continuous volatility can create profitability challenges. Creating predictable and controllable relationships of supply and demand through vertical integration can create considerable value, and when profitability does migrate along the supply chain, the business is always positioned to capture it.

Family businesses are also good at creating value through diversification. Often, individual family members run the separate businesses, and they can achieve a rare level of independence from one another. Conventional wisdom holds that diversifying outside of a core industry will require the acquisition of new knowledge and competencies, which can be a distraction to senior management. The ability of families to delegate responsibility and authority to individual family members seems particularly well suited to this challenge. At the same time, shared ownership and governance allow the family to foster the effective capital integration and interdependence of disparate, combined business ventures. Capital allocation decisions are often made more readily and strategically. Diversification that appears haphazard in conventional thinking often serves an underlying risk-reduction strategy for family owners. By diversifying across a number of markets, families avoid having all their eggs in one business basket, and reduce their exposure to risks within a single industry. Diversification enables families to remain constant to the long-term view.

The unusual success of family businesses at both vertical integration and diversification strategies is the result of combining their focus on costs and profits with their concentrated control. There is one more important way that family businesses are particularly well adapted to these strategies. Because many families seek to keep value in their businesses, they can use vertical integration and diversification strategies for tax advantage. Often, profits in one business are offset by expenses or losses in another, or tax shelters in one business are fully leveraged in combination with another. In these ways, value can accumulate sheltered from the dilution of taxes, and over the long run more profits can be retained. The key enabling component of this is a common ownership interest in building and retaining value in the business, rather than pursuing returns through liquidity. This is a very common component of family businesses that is more rarely found in other businesses.

Unconventional strategies common to family businesses

The ability of family-owned businesses to focus on the long term while maintaining concentrated control enables considerable strategic agility and ingenuity. Family businesses can be more adaptive and creative in pursuing competitive advantages. Their concentrated control enables them to act quickly and then to be more patient. Family businesses can take short-term risks that have long-term payoffs, which other companies tend to avoid. They can 'go against the grain' in tough economic times, buying market share or penetrating new markets that are temporarily out of favor. The ability to act fast and pursue diversification strategies disfavored by conventional wisdom allows family businesses to add value opportunistically during bad economic cycles. Their patience, in turn, allows them to create long-term value from temporarily disfavored industry segments.

Family businesses tend to combine patient capital with an idiosyncratic knowledge from deep business experience. Their collective business memory is transmitted across generations, and they often approach recession cycles differently. While other businesses tend to cut back investment reflexively during industry downturns, family businesses often have experience with cycles that enables them to maintain optimal investment levels for both weathering the storm and emerging with strategic advantage. Over long periods of time, as cycles are repeated, the value of this combination of patience and knowledge is compounded and can create both significant market penetration and greater long-term returns.

Family businesses also tend to operate in unusual market niches. They commonly do dangerous or 'dirty' work, and dominate many hazardous industries, such as waste disposal. This is a good example of how family companies often accumulate knowledge, experience, and specially adapted equipment and technology. They seem particularly adept at transmitting the knowledge internally and maintaining industry relations effectively over long periods of time. The embedded collective memory, born of long family business histories, is an important advantage in specialized markets, as are long-standing industry relationships that foster trust. These characteristics are common to many older family businesses and their approach to the stakeholders of their companies.

Understanding how cultural elements define family business strategy

The strategies of family businesses are often unique and unusual. Their origins are at times obscure, and seem to lack business sense. A thorough understanding of how and why family business strategies are effective often requires a careful exploration of the family and business history and culture. One important approach to this question is to investigate how family vision and values underlie business strategy and development. Often, the shared purpose that develops between the family enterprise and its owners is culturally defined and framed by an economic relationship.

In family businesses, there is no single, successful model for how this relationship should be structured or this purpose defined. Most often, the structure and goals have a historical and cultural base, and become embedded over time. Often, these are a reflection of underlying values, and express a particular combination of attitudes or core beliefs in the family. These core beliefs relate to the relationship of the family to the business and vice versa, and they often become structurally embedded in the first two generations. Families create many distinct structural solutions, adapting to their unique combination of core beliefs, and often must continue to adapt as the relationship between the family and the business changes.

Understanding how family culture is related to business strategies and structures can help business-owning families better understand their underlying ownership purpose. Answering a number of questions can serve to illustrate the core beliefs of the ownership family. The first question to ask is whether the family puts the business or the family first? Business-first families tend to see the business as a sacred institution, with a life and purpose of its own that must be preserved and maintained. A family-first attitude views the purpose of the business as benefiting the family.

The founder usually establishes whether the family serves the business or the business serves the family. This is often an expression of their personality, and whether family life or work life is more important to them. These attitudes of the founder can profoundly influence succession strategies and decisions, and translate into particular management or ownership structures. They can also engender very different embedded value propositions, reflecting a full spectrum of payout rates and growth potential. The founder's attitudes about wealth can profoundly effect this equation, which, in turn, will dictate strategic parameters for the business.

Another key question is whether the family perceives the business as glue for the family or a threat to family unity. This question has particular resonance in the second generation, where siblings have to decide whether the business is a source of coherence or conflict. Family ownership's core beliefs in this area profoundly influence the development of governance and ownership structures. Some families build structures that create a high degree of engagement among family members around business issues, while others seek to insulate business decisions from family dynamics. A wide range of structural adaptations can result from this, including everything from voting trusts to family councils. In addition, ownership demands for liquidity are usually a direct reflection of basic attitudes about whether the business functions as glue or a threat to the family. A lack of coherency creates higher liquidity demands, and a family effect that raises the cost of capital. These many variables can profoundly impact the strategic parameters imposed on the business.

The final question that reveals an ownership family's core beliefs relates to the nature of leadership, and whether team leadership or individual leadership is seen as more effective. This attitude is also usually established in the first two generations, when the family finds out how it makes decisions most effectively. Some families work best by empowering decision-making teams that lead from consensus, while other families find giving a single individual responsibility and authority for decisions is more productive. Embedded in this question is the link between accountability and authority. Some families believe that individual leadership is the only way to create accountability, while other families have a hard time holding family members accountable and prefer to place control in a team. This dynamic of accountability can have a profound impact on leadership structures, and whether teams or individuals lead and how authority is granted. This, in turn, profoundly affects processes of strategy development and selection.

Each family has a different combination of core beliefs. Ownership attitudes are forged in the unique experience of an individual family working to build a particular business. The requirements and capabilities of the business and the culture of the family are wrapped up in a single history, which engenders a family vision of the business. This vision is an expression of the family's unique combination of core beliefs, and it defines how the relationship between the business and family can be most successful. Culture and values are the foundation of this vision, and this vision, in turn, engenders the structures for ownership, leadership, and governance, which are created to maintain the system. This embedding of core beliefs in structure defines the family's vision for ownership and leadership, and becomes a driving force in strategy.

The competitive advantage of family firms

The ability of family businesses to successfully pursue unconventional strategies is their key competitive advantage. Most companies must comply with the narrow expectations and short-term measures imposed by external capital markets. The need to meet market expectations for quarterly numbers can dictate many short-term decisions in a typical company, even when this has negative long-term implications. Markets will also frown on departures from conventional business wisdom, creating disincentives for creativity. Family companies are often free of the pressures engendered by market expectations, and can break from the constraints of convention to pursue more productive, counterintuitive strategies. They can do what makes sense in the long term, pursuing the 'right' decisions, even when they bear short-term consequences, or seem 'wrong' to everyone else. Family businesses can be different. They can stretch convention, and their wider latitude in business adaptation becomes a primary competitive advantage and enables their better long-term business performance.

Many characteristics of family businesses are viewed negatively by conventional wisdom. Among the common liabilities attributed to family business systems are nepotism, constrained capital, insular and unorthodox strategies, and family dynamics driving business decisions. All these negative assumptions can be turned on their heads, however, with closer examination. Nepotism can lead to more systematic preparation of leadership, and the development of a high degree of idiosyncratic knowledge transmission. Capital constraints can lead to greater discipline, lower overheads, and the selection of less capital-intense strategies with lower risk. Concentrated control supporting unconventional strategies may seem insular and unorthodox, but it allows the productive pursuit of out-of-favor industries or strategies like vertical integration and diversification. Finally, convention dismisses the influence of family issues on business decisions as rational or productive, and yet the direct link between ownership and business interests is essential to the competitive advantage of family businesses.

There are many cases where, upon initial examination, the influence of the family on the business seems to manifest in 'trivial' ways. Operating units are divided according to the number of succeeding family managers, or new operations are located where family members want to live. Decisions about who comes into the business or who controls ownership are often the result of personal interactions, and can be related more to inter-generation relationships and personality conflict than to competency. Sometimes, payout rates are changed to quiet dissent or capital is restructured to buy out dissident family members. Some family members are even kept on the job with diminished responsibilities when others would have been fired, just to hold them and their branch of the family in the fold. Family businesses do regularly accommodate family issues in making business decisions, but far from trivial, this is done with the recognition that family disharmony will have a direct impact on the business.

Everyone is familiar with how family disputes raise costs or even break up productive business systems. But rarely is the value of maintaining unified ownership recognized. Families themselves recognize the balance between accommodation and productive business decisions. They know that the system must balance family and business demands, and indeed their long combined histories often provide examples of how this is done productively in their business and family. Understanding this embedded relationship often requires digging into culture and values. The pattern of success in family businesses reflects the development of a symbiotic relationship between ownership and business. This symbiosis is rooted in culture and can develop in innumerable, sometimes 'trivial,' ways. Yet, maintaining it across time is the very foundation of family business success.

Family businesses, with their discrete ownership groups, can be particularly well adapted to maintaining the alignment of ownership and business interests within strategy. They recognize more readily that strategy is a choice, and there is no single 'best' strategy. Many interests and issues need to be balanced in strategy selection, and often the most critical element of strategy success is patience. The characteristic concentrated control found in the governance of family firms makes them highly effective at pursuing unconventional strategies. They can accommodate pressures within the system, balance interests and objectives, and create strategic confidence and resolve. The long-term relationships and shared knowledge found within families and their companies tend to breed trust and enable highly productive pursuit of the unconventional.

Conclusion

For all their potential weaknesses, families are still the social unit with the greatest ability to engender mutual trust in situations of shared economic interests. Family ties combined with a business culture can help provide a clearer understanding of shared financial stakes, and this understanding, in turn, is often supported by a shared foundation of values. Family owners know how to relate what is best for the business to what is best for them. They know that maintaining this link is essential to optimizing their shared economic interests. For these reasons, families in business are particularly adept at pursuing effective ongoing governance adaptations that maintain simple, responsive structures and concentrated control. The strategic advantage of family businesses is built on a cultural foundation of shared values that enables trust and concentrated control to be maintained and coupled with a long-term approach to strategy. This foundation enables the patient, informed pursuit of unconventional strategies that can produce above average long-term financial results for family companies.

When family owners maintain a foundation of trust and mutually under-stood economic interest, they create competitive advantages for their businesses. When these advantages are maintained over long periods of time – and in family business this often means for generations – considerable accumulation and consolidation of competitive advantage is possible. As families and their businesses grow, maintaining their foundation for success takes increasingly complex planning and ongoing engagement between ownership and the business. Adaptations of governance structures and plan-ning processes are often necessary to maintain historic symbiotic relationships across time. The sustained strategic flexibility, consistency, and creativity of family businesses are remarkable, and it is these characteristics that differentiate them from other businesses and enables their higher levels of financial performance.

3
Strategic Planning – It Starts With the Family

John L. Ward

S trategic planning has become a common best practice in most organizations. Businesses of all shapes and sizes, public and private, pursue this practice, many with a high degree of sophistication. The process of strategic planning involves assessing the external and internal economic environments of the business. Many complex analytical metrics can be used to assess the relative strengths or weaknesses of the general economy, the firm's industry, its competitors, and its own internal resources and operations. All these metrics are used to test the value propositions of the business and create a picture of their future strategic potential within the market. These findings, in turn, help direct capital investment decisions and near-term business planning. Indeed, the processes of strategic planning are completely embedded in the standard management practices of today.

Most businesses develop their planning processes through a logical evolution over time. They usually begin by planning and tracking budgets, with the goal of more accurately predicting short-term outcomes. Initially, business planning tends to focus on internal operations, their output and efficiency.

As this planning becomes more financially sophisticated and gains accuracy, there is an increasing desire to push the planning horizon out into the future. Pushing planning out in time, however, tends to generate fluctuations in the accuracy of forecasts, and this causes businesses to seek a deeper understanding of the many economic factors that impact their financial performance. Acquiring this knowledge enables business leaders to more accurately anticipate outcomes and make better informed business decisions. Ultimately, it allows them to apply strategic thinking to questions of capital investment and future business development.

The organic evolution of planning processes described above is commonly found in many organizations. In business, strategic planning is most often the end result of a long process of knowledge acquisition by management. Managers begin with budgets and then gradually learn to make use of increasingly sophisticated insights for planning. As their understanding of the business progresses over time, it begins to reshape management's conception of the business's strategic potential. This, in turn, helps to hone decisions, and refocus business planning on the most distinctive and sustainable competitive advantages of the firm in its marketplace. As management acquires knowledge and its planning grows more strategic, the board of directors is usually involved, reviewing assumptions and approving plans. Often, it is the board that pushes management to pursue greater knowledge acquisition and more sophisticated planning.

Fully mature business planning involves both management and the board in a strategic planning process. Generally, best practice holds that management drives the creation of strategy, subject to board approval. Boards often conduct their own level of strategic planning related to capital planning and major resource allocation decisions, but it is typically management that does the bulk of planning development for the business. Managers create the internal and external assessments, and make recommendations regarding strategy and tactics in the business plan. The board must review these plans and make sure that they are rigorous and well aligned with the capital strategies of the business. Ultimately, the goal is to create sustainable value for the shareholders by preparing the business to compete in the future.

This current paradigm of best practice planning begs the question: What should be the role of ownership in business planning? Conventional wisdom has viewed the dispersed ownership model found in capital markets as the most rational method for organizing ownership. It is thought that the buying and selling of shares in an open market provides direct checks and balances on management and the board. Dispersed shareholders 'vote with their feet,' and the decisions they make to buy or sell in the market are the ultimate measure of success or failure. In this model, owners have no direct role in planning, but they do pass ultimate judgment on the strategy and strategic potential of the business by deciding to buy, hold, or sell.

The dynamic of this paradigm, however, can have a distorting effect on strategy selection or execution. A business can have a brilliant planning process and an infallible strategy, but if it does not align with ownership expectations, the business will not succeed in the market. Equity markets can be notoriously fickle and irrational, paying up value that does not exist or dumping solid performance to seek out quicker gains. Conventional wisdom says that the market will squeeze out its own erratic performance over time, but in the interim the strategy and planning of many successful public companies has been shaped by prevailing market expectations. The lack of a direct ownership role in planning is the chief weakness of this market-driven paradigm. Too often, strategy becomes spin, as managers and boards try to 'sell' their concepts of the company and what it will be.

Family companies, particularly privately held ones, have the considerable advantage of discrete, coherent ownership groups that can be directly involved in planning processes and strategy formation. This critical advantage allows family companies to choose a strategy because it is right for the business and ownership, rather than because of its spin potential in the market. Family owners often cannot 'vote with their feet,' and their lack of liquidity can be a motivating force for maintaining close ownership control and direct involvement in planning. Understanding the strategic prospects of the business is essential to the future of the family, and making decisions that are strategically right for the business and the family can compound to great effect in the future. Family businesses have a greater potential for alignment between ownership, boards, and management in strategic planning processes, which, in turn, translates into greater strategic clarity, agility and commitment.

How strategic planning in family business is different

Family businesses develop planning processes in the same organic way that other businesses do. They start with annual financial planning, and gradually develop the use of more sophisticated tools and planning techniques over time. Long before a formal planning process is created, however, most family businesses have the well-developed strategic foundation of a shared owner-ship and business vision. Often, this vision is first embodied in the founder, and formed from his or her perceptions about the relationship between the family and the business. Included and balanced within this vision are the perceived needs and capabilities of both the family and the business. The potential of the business and the ability of ownership to optimize that potential are both part of the equation. Over time, changes in the family and its business tend to drive a continuous need to re-evaluate this perceived strategic foundation. Far from being a weakness, this organic need for the regular renewal of a shared ownership and business vision makes family businesses both more stable and responsive.

How does this dynamic work? Initially, the mutual adaptations between ownership families and their businesses happen organically. At the entrepreneurial stage there is no barrier between ownership and management – they are one and the same. Their success is mutually defined and dependent. Creating value is a function of sweat equity, personal values and business potential. Founding entrepreneurs know their businesses and their families intimately, and they often deal with succession by creating structures that are carefully adapted to the perceived strengths and weaknesses of both. This leads to myriad adaptations, including some that seem frivolous from a business perspective. Families routinely tailor business structures to divide responsibilities to match a given number of family successors or family branches. These structures appear to respond to family needs rather than business needs, and yet they are often highly successful because they tend to concentrate authority and focus energy.

While structural adaptations can be as varied as the families that create them, they all tend to share the common characteristic of a unified and balanced vision. Most often, this vision is first engendered by their founders and is based on their particular perspective of the family and the business. In creating structures, founders naturally anticipate future points of stress or conflict in the family business system, and seek to compensate by adopting structures that can cultivate mutual strengths and suppress potential weaknesses. They also seek to define and transmit culture and values that are shared mutually by the business and the family, and this common foundation of structure and culture in family businesses can be remarkably stable.

Stability, however, does not always translate into long-term continuity. This is particularly true in the competitive world of business, where the need to change can become a matter of survival. As firms grow and mature, they inevitably face challenges of scale and competition within their industries, and must adapt to the potential life cycles of business. In family enterprises, family members age, generations succeed, and the life cycles of the family also become superimposed on the system. Conventional wisdom views issues of family succession as tangential to business continuity and strategic planning, which it says should be focused purely on industry dynamics and the sustainable competitive advantages of the business. The simultaneous and unrelated pressures inherent in family and business life cycles would seem to complicate strategic transitions, and yet family businesses achieve a higher degree of continuity than other businesses. Conventional thinking cannot account for this phenomenon.

Far from being a weakness, however, family succession may be a strategic strength of the system. New generations of ownership and management have to think in new ways. With each generation succession, the number of shareholders in a family company tends to grow. This can lead to an increasing number of family owners being active in management, but it also tends to increase the percentage of ownership held by non-active family shareholders outside the business. As a result, the percentage of ownership held by management tends to decline by generation. Often, ownership, management and governance structures must adapt to these changes, causing a regular process of systemic renewal. New relationships between ownership and management must be cultivated, roles and responsibilities defined. This often leads the family to revisit the embedded shareholder value proposition of the business and its long-term strategic potential. This process, in turn, serves to renew the mutual commitment between the family and the business, and can recast or reinforce shared expectations for the future.

Conventional wisdom sees family pressures on the business system as a distraction. Many experts believe that businesses must focus on the strategic pressures of industry trends and competition in adapting their response to the market. What is so often ignored is the inherent tendency of business systems to resist change, to rationalize rather than renew. Family enterprises also face this problem of 'business as usual,' but each generational succession comes as a new opportunity for strategic renewal. The challenges of maintaining effective family ownership control are clear, but the opportunities these challenges engender are rarely appreciated. Most often, in older family business systems, a foundation of mutual identification, of shared culture and values, provides the family and its enterprise with a sense of continuity that enables adaptation and change. Rather than being a distraction, involved family ownership is a powerful agent of strategic renewal.

Transforming cultural vision into strategy

No business has only one strategic option, and strategy selection is a highly subjective process. Family businesses can be particularly agile in the selection of strategies, and yet they are often highly focused on a particular set of strategic parameters. Embedded structures, leadership biases and established shareholder value propositions can all become strategic givens that must be accounted for in planning. The ownership vision, born out of a long, successful relationship between the family and the business, shapes what strategies are seen and preferred by leadership. Many of these preferences are unconscious and implicit reflections of values and culture within the thought process of leaders. Their strategic thinking moves naturally from beliefs to concepts to strategies and tactics. Ownership vision is part of the unique, idiosyncratic knowledge transmitted in family business cultures, and it becomes so embedded that it is a major directing force in strategy.

The development of strategic planning in family businesses can help make the connections between ownership vision and strategic business potential more explicit. This becomes particularly critical over time, as market conditions or scale impact the business, or generation successions impact the family. The goals and aspirations of a family can change over time, as can the strategic potential of their business. The family business system must be capable of accounting for these changes and adapting its business strategies in ways that continue to align business goals with ownership vision. Over time, as an ownership family and its business change scale, there is an ever-increasing need for better planning processes. To be most effective, planning must assure that the business and its ownership remain directly linked and mutually informed in strategy development and selection.

A good business planning process can help the family understand the evolving conditions of the market, and the strategic constraints these impose on their business. At the same time, an active renewal of a coherent ownership vision is required with each generational succession of the family. Family ownership groups tend to grow exponentially with each generation, making this renewal of ownership vision a more and more complex challenge, which increasingly requires a formal planning process of its own. Underlying this challenge are changes of culture that can impact the core beliefs of the family over time.

Larger ownership groups tend to have less direct management involvement and their values regarding the business become more diverse. Core beliefs can evolve with each generation. The family may change its perspective on whether the business or family comes first, or whether owning the business is glue or a threat, or whether team or individual leadership is perceived as best. The family dynamic of succeeding sibling and cousin generations can develop in ways very different from what the older generation envisioned, and each generation must rise to the challenge of productively shaping its collective vision.

The core beliefs of ownership families can remain quite stable for long periods of time, particularly when they are well articulated and actively transmitted across generations. Good business performance also helps maintain symbiotic family cultures. But inevitably, all family business systems face the challenges of change, either in the family or the business (or sometimes both), and must create a process for cultural transmission, transformation and renewal in the family. Ownership's attitudes about wealth creation versus extraction, acceptable risk parameters, growth targets, leadership selection and accountability tend to evolve over time. Family life cycles and generation successions drive this process of shifting core beliefs, as do changes in business performance. If the family is to remain effectively linked to its business, a common, coherent ownership vision must be articulated. This takes active engagement and an increasingly sophisticated ownership planning process with each generation succession.

Families can be quite adept at achieving cultural continuity in change. Often, this involves translating the historical culture and values and giving them new meaning in the current day. It can also involve an ongoing evolution of governance structures adapted to the changing scale of the ownership group and its business. As families and their businesses grow in size, the need to directly link the process of vision renewal in ownership to strategic planning in business becomes ever more essential. Maintaining a symbiotic relationship between a business and its family ownership requires them to be mutually informed and directed by a common vision. Governance structures that effectively link the family ownership with business leadership serve to better align ownership vision and strategic potential. Effective planning processes that integrate family and business planning create the best strategic thinking and enable the most effective strategy selection and execution.

Parallel planning in family business

A new best practice paradigm is taking shape in family business today. This involves parallel business and family planning (Carlock and Ward, 2001). Parallel planning lays out a sequenced framework of planning processes that unify family and business planning and assure the alignment of ownership and business strategy. In parallel planning, standard business planning processes and tools are combined with family planning processes in a specific sequence of targeted outcomes. These planning processes happen separately and in parallel, and then are brought together at three distinct decision points. The goal of this process is to align the family and management in a single strategic vision, which expresses mutually understood expectations about the future. The ultimate product of this process is a strategic plan capable of optimizing the long-term economic value of the enterprise.

Maintaining the symbiotic relationship between family ownership and their business over time can become quite challenging. For the family and business to succeed, planning needs to account for and balance the changing demands of the family and the business. An effective process involves both building shared knowledge and generating mutual accountability. When well executed, parallel planning processes allow even large family business systems to maintain a high degree of adaptability while ensuring that ownership and business vision and strategy are aligned. This requires an ongoing planning process capable of continuous ownership and business reassessment. A well conceived and executed strategic business plan is only a first step, and a continuous process of engagement and reassessment is necessary to enable the optimal economic performance of the family business system over time.

As in the development of business planning, many of the elements of parallel planning tend to develop organically. Often, early ownership succession decisions dictate how family control of the business is structured and held. They also tend to establish embedded shareholder value propositions that dictate how ownership interests are rewarded economically. Usually, these structures are not explicitly related to business strategy, but once historically embedded, they tend to become an important strategic context for decisions. Over time, the business operates within this context and gradually develops strategic planning as a natural progression of its experience and capabilities. Planning in the family tends to lag behind business planning, developing more slowly and less systematically. Family planning tends to be reactive more than proactive, and sometimes only happens when existing arrangements are challenged by changes in the business or the family.

Family leaders are often reluctant to revisit ownership structures or recast the economic purpose of an embedded shareholder value proposition. Family business leaders tend to fear mixing family dynamics and business planning, and many throw up a wall between ownership and management working processes. Business leaders naturally have more authority and control over management processes than family ones, and many family managers see ownership issues as a distraction from their more important obligation of running the business effectively. Over time, though, changes in the family ownership inevitably create challenges to business continuity that must be addressed. Generational successions lead to changes in family scale, transfer tax issues, and the evolution of investment objectives. Long-established payout rates and levels of ownership liquidity can become challenging to maintain, and eventually an active process for engaging with family owner-ship and renewing their commitment must be developed.

For the reasons above, planning in the family is often done reluctantly, in response to emerging issues. Parallel planning argues that a planned, ongoing process of ownership engagement is more likely to achieve success for both the family and the business. Processes established before issues emerge have greater potential to enable constructive resolution than ad hoc processes created in the midst of debate. While parallel planning is rarely a linear process, and its many planning elements tend to develop organically at different rates, an understanding of the overall framework can help family business leaders proactively pursue its different parts over time. Incremental, systematic development of this framework should become part of every family business's strategic planning process. While different elements may develop sooner or later, the systemic goal remains the same – making strategic decisions that reflect the dual realities of the potential of the business and the level of family ownership commitment to reinvestment.

The parallel planning process

There are three stages of parallel planning. In each stage, planning work is done simultaneously and separately in family ownership and senior management, and then their outcomes are brought together. The merging of ownership and management perspectives helps create a decision-filtering process at the end of each stage. The goal is to align the family and the business at each stage, and arrive at consensus before moving on to the next step. Changes in family attitudes or the strategic potential of the business can cause the process to move backward before it can move forward again. Many family businesses also have existing elements to plug into the framework. For example, the ownership side might have a shareholder agreement and the business side a fully developed strategic plan. Coordinating and aligning existing elements often involves going backward in the parallel planning process. The framework is presented as a progression, but elements themselves are often completed in a patchwork fashion.

The first stage in the process involves the family exploring its business philosophy and core values. This is done through family meetings, not business meetings, and the process should provide for the active involvement of all family owners, inside and outside the business, small and large stakeholders alike. The objective of this process is to generate a common family vision for the future. This vision should articulate the core values of the family, and set out future expectations for business growth and ownership structure and succession. Included in this vision should be a clear understanding of the impact of taxation on ownership successions, and how this may impact future family demands on capital. The goal of this family work should be to generate a written Family Commitment,[1] which can express

---

[1] For more details on ingredients of Family Commitment, Strategic Commitment, Shared Future Vision and Family Continuity Plan, see Carlock and Ward (2001).

both a consensus of ownership views to management and a commitment among family owners to remain active and engaged.

On the business side, the corresponding parallel planning process of management involves an exploration of the firm's business philosophy and long-term objectives. Management seeks to articulate a business vision, which can be communicated to the family through a written Strategic Commitment. This Strategic Commitment should characterize management's view of the business's future potential size, profitability, and growth rates. It should also provide a strategic view of the industry and a risk profile for the business. A strategic business plan will typically contain all of these high-level outcomes, though they are rarely broken out in a formal document. Sometimes, after business vision statements are crafted, they become enshrined and forgotten, but the best strategic planning annually revisits, questions and renews the highest level strategic assumptions. A business vision should not be a platitude, and a current, formal Strategic Commitment by management can function as a strong directing vision.

After ownership and management have completed their parallel processes in this first stage, the Family and Strategic Commitments are exchanged and reviewed. The family must understand management's business vision, and managers must understand the family's ownership vision. In most family businesses, some family leaders have been involved in both parts of the parallel process, and they often serve to keep ownership and management commitments mutually informed. At this point, it is important to conduct a careful review and identify any misalignment in these visions. A dialogue of participants from both sides should also take place. Often, this dialogue engenders critical thinking, and assumptions on both sides are called into question, explored and refined. Out of this process comes a written Shared

Future Vision, which reflects ownership and management's shared assumptions and objectives for the future.

In many family businesses, this mutual commitment is already deeply embedded and easily achieved. Often, this process is one of drawing out and articulating a vision that has long been contained within the shared history and culture of the business and family. Making this understanding more explicit can powerfully renew the mutual commitment of family and business, and provide a greater ability to adopt new strategies that have higher potential and can achieve better long-term objectives. But not all family businesses can readily achieve a Shared Future Vision. For many a prolonged negotiation process may be necessary to resolve disputed expectations.

Most often, misalignment is the result of different visions for the business from the inside and the outside. This can reflect a family divide between family owner/managers inside the business and non-active family owner/ investors outside the business. As families and businesses grow, senior management teams tend to include an increasing number of non-family professionals, leading sometimes to inside/outside divides that separate family owner/investors and professional managers. When the future expectations from the inside and outside do not match, there are profound implications for strategy, and resolving these differences through mutual engagement and negotiation is essential.

The negotiation of a Shared Future Vision can happen in many ways, and would typically involve the family ownership, the board of directors, and senior management. It would often include special meetings as well as the active use of all existing governance structures. Sometimes, new governance practices are adopted to better facilitate this process of negotiation. Resolution can take time, and will necessarily involve give and take. If differences in expectations cannot be resolved, then this becomes a limiting factor that must be accounted for in strategy. Senior managers may need to be replaced or dissident family owners bought out to enable consensus. Sometimes, the adaptation of governance structures is also necessary in order to provide for more effective ongoing dialogue.

It is important to reach a clear Shared Future Vision, and to revisit and renew this commitment regularly. Market conditions change, and successions in management and ownership can alter perspectives and goals. A formal annual review as part of ongoing planning processes is advised, and serves to keep the concepts fresh and bring issues to the surface. The objective is to maintain a vision agreement that is current for both management and the family ownership. The ultimate outcome of this first stage in parallel planning is the creation of a Vision Fit Filter, a planning tool which incorporates the shared commitments of ownership and management. This filter can be used as an initial screen for identifying high-level strategies that align the business potential envisioned by management and the ownership goals of the family.

In the second stage of parallel planning, the family develops a Family Enterprise Continuity Plan, while management develops a Business Strategy Plan. In its planning, the family must resolve issues of family participation, family leadership development and succession, and comprehensive ownership planning. For its part, management pursues detailed strategic planning processes with the objective of clearly defining the strategic potential of the business. This ongoing work is parallel and often proceeds at different paces. Both tracks are seeking solutions appropriate to the articulated commitments. Ultimately these two plans come together, assuring their alignment for the next step.

Creating the Family Enterprise Continuity Plan involves many potential elements, and requires sustained effort over long periods of time. First, issues of family member participation in governance and management must be resolved. This means deciding how individuals will be chosen, developed, and involved, as well as setting ground rules for meetings and standards for communication. Some families draft written Participation Agreements, to govern these areas. The second focus of family planning is family leadership succession and next-generation career development. Critical, future leadership competencies should be identified and a proactive process for the development of successors created. Attention to cultivating productive next-generation relationships is critical, and many families create written Codes of Conduct or Career Development Plans to clarify a common policy for all family members. Development of ownership planning is the third focus area. This includes estate planning, resolving issues of ownership succession and structures, and the articulation of investment expectations. Many families create written ownership agreements, and/or develop formal family governance out of this process. This is discussed in more detail in Chapter 10.

While the family does its work, management is busy developing a more detailed business strategic plan. The planning team uses the many conventional tools and techniques of strategic planning to assess the business and its industry. Management should begin by reaching a common understanding of the competitive position and potential of the business in its industry. This includes analyzing market share trends, and the competitive potential of current value propositions in the market. After the company's market position is clear, management conducts a thorough analysis of internal capabilities in finance, marketing, and business organization. This helps clarify the strategic capabilities within the firm, and should identify both strengths and weaknesses. Finally, management conducts a thorough external analysis, characterizing current trends in both the general economy and the operating industry, and seeks to identify both opportunities and threats within the market environment. All of this analysis is pulled together by management in order to accurately articulate the strategic potential of the business.

The board of directors and the family should review management's characterization of the firm's strategic potential, and these three groups should reach a general consensus supporting this assessment. Any questions about strategic potential must be resolved before further planning can take place, and if consensus does not exist, a facilitated process at this stage is sometimes necessary.

In the third stage of parallel planning, management chooses those strategies with the greatest potential for success that are consistent with the objectives of ownership. This is the final step in their strategic planning process, and these recommendations are reviewed and approved by the board of directors. At this stage, a final alignment process involves the family ownership. All businesses must invest for the future, and reinvestment levels in family businesses are often directly tied to levels of shareholder payouts for liquidity. The family must understand its current payout and reinvestment levels, and their impacts on potential for future business growth. A good process will engage ownership in an exploration of a range of reinvestment scenarios and risk profiles related to optimizing the potential of the business.

Ultimately, the reinvestment decision defines the common ground between the strategic business potential and the family ownership's commitment to reinvestment. Clear expectations about levels of shareholder return and business performance need to be laid out. This creates clear criteria for choosing strategic initiatives and tactics, and assures that the entire family business system is aligned to achieve the same goals. Achieving this level of alignment gives family businesses their chief strategic advantages – clarity, consistency, patience, and adaptability. When strategic decisions are well aligned, tactics can be more flexible, creative and unconventional. With good planning, family businesses can pursue value in the most effective ways across long periods of time. This is the foundation of their unusual financial success and continuity.

Leveraging the competitive advantage of family businesses

Family ownership can create competitive advantages for their business. If well organized and committed, the economic stake of ownership can be directly tied to strategies that optimize the business. The level of connection between long-term ownership goals and maximizing business potential is unusually high in family businesses. Their concentrated ownership control allows greater strategic agility and patience, but maintaining these advantages can become increasingly difficult as the family and the business mature. Decisions simultaneously affect the family and business, and allocating capital between reinvestment and shareholder distributions is a constant dilemma. No fixed formula can substitute for a rigorous mutual understanding, or, when necessary, thoughtful negotiation.

Businesses must adapt to the changing strategic potential of their market or their value proposition. All businesses need ongoing reinvestment, and for each one there is an optimal level of capital investment tied to their ability to grow and cover the cost of capital. Over time, family owners tend to become more economically dependent on the income stream from their businesses, and as this happens, they also tend to grow more risk-averse. Alignment of family and business capital needs requires the two sides of the system to stay mutually informed about the future through coordinated planning. Decisions must realistically balance the family's economic aspirations with the strategic potential and capital needs of the business. Effective strategic planning will account for both, and reveal when the expectations or needs of one side are out of alignment with the other. Family owners can be directly involved in planning, and this access to knowledge and opportunity for input is what allows family businesses to balance their capital requirements and steadily pursue optimization of business results.

All family business systems face the same key issues of management successions, ownership transitions, and the ongoing renewal of effective governance structures and business strategies. Practices of parallel planning that involve the family ownership, the board, and management are essential to resolving these issues in ways that promote family cohesion and optimal business performance. Active engagement of the family is the key to building trust in the system, and a positive family effect. Coherent ownership families add considerable value by providing patient capital at a lower cost, and the entire business system benefits from the predictability of unified control with a clear purpose. Achieving these results, however, is a moving target, particularly as families grow, and generations succeed one another. Historically, the connection between family and business is often cultural, and becomes embodied in individuals and cast in structure. But over time this connection must be renewed, and often this requires a willingness to change and adapt to the current circumstances of the family and the business.

Conclusion

Family work is essential to the success of the family business system. Achieving optimal business performance requires an active ownership planning process that ties directly back to business planning and promotes continuous dialogue and alignment. Effective parallel planning informs the family of strategic business issues in advance of decision-making, and enables even large ownership groups to be far more responsive and supportive of business initiatives. Parallel planning also serves to directly inform management of family ownership's financial objectives and risk tolerance, which should be a key part of strategic thinking. When all these elements are combined, family businesses maintain their higher performance and enhanced long-term value creation.

Reference

Carlock, R.S. and Ward, J.L. 2001. *Strategic Planning for the Family Business*. London: Palgrave.

4
How Family Business Culture is Different

Colleen Lief and Daniel Denison

ontrary to the general perception of family firms as small, backward mom and pop stores, some of the world's largest and best-known companies are family controlled. As noted in the Preface, recent studies of the largest listed corporations confirm the counterintuitive notion that family businesses are more profitable than non-family firms. While the most sensational stories on family enterprises feature incompetent successors and a stodgy, stick-to-our-guns rigid glorification of the past, the reality is far different. In a study conducted by the IMD-Lombard Odier Darier Hentsch (LODH) Family Business Research Center, family firms were found to constitute 26% of the 50 Best European Performers as selected by *Business Week* (Fairlamb, 2003).

Further, contrary to the widely held idea that family firms are so rooted in history that they forget about the present and are unprepared for the future, family companies have been observed to demonstrate focused entrepreneurial tendencies and a higher threshold for extended return on longer investment time horizons. The very element which one might intuitively conclude would limit a family firm's interest in new product and market development actually frees management to take measured, intelligent risks where they see opportunity. Much has been written about the role of successors as stewards of the family legacy through the family business and as guardians of capital. However, the arena of investment and entrepreneurship is an area in which enterprising families demonstrate their capacity for balancing apparent opposites (to be discussed in more detail later). While stewardship is critical to the survival of the firm and the wealth of family members, innovation and business development are the keys to extending the life and retaining the competitiveness of the business. It is not a question of current success or long-term viability. The answer must be both.

The thorough knowledge of the firm and its industry possessed by many successors lends insights into creative, unexpected choices for investment. The fact that family business managers are dealing with their own money and the inheritance of their children and are not as subject to the quarterly whims of Wall Street allows for more patient capital. While the gravity of this reality could equally be expected to make decision-makers timid, it has been observed that family firms generally respond in quite the opposite way. They may act intelligently but boldly at critical junctures, knowing that the benefit or loss will accrue directly to the family. The knowledge that they are acting on behalf of the larger family group that depends on the company for its lifeblood spurs family managers to render decisions intended to steadily contribute to the family's incremental and long-term wealth (James, 1999). The goal is for each generation to grow the company's value as a memorial to the founder's vision but also in financial support of a growing family group. The mandate to leave behind a business stronger and better than the one they inherited is a powerful motivator in imaginative, reasoned decision-making.

So why do family companies perform better? A variety of arguments have been offered, but one of the most compelling involves a link between superior financial performance and superior corporate culture. When competitors in an industry have products, suppliers and even customers and strategies in common, culture can be an important – and sometimes the only – differentiating factor. For family firms, culture can be a distinct and unique source of advantage that naturally springs from their unique history, ownership and organizational dynamics.

Peters and Waterman (1982), in their book *In Search of Excellence*, presented culture for the first time as that intangible something that could be harnessed and managed and used as a source of competitive power. The recognition that business organizations have individual personalities and ways of expressing their fundamental philosophies, owes much to the pioneering work of Edgar Schein (1985), among others. What became increasingly clear was that what a company truly believes about itself and the world is manifested in its observable traditions, organizational structure and physical symbols.

Constant reconsideration of a company's value proposition is certainly essential to a vital, healthy enterprise. Especially in times of economic contraction when market and competitive variables have been fully addressed and optimized, looking inward may be the next most logical place to search for competitive advantage and organizational coherence. A thorough understanding of an organization's cultural character may be management's last, best weapon.

Whether judged to be positive or negative, barely acknowledged or actively managed, culture in corporations exists. A corporation's character can no longer be ignored in understanding how best to leverage a company's inherent strengths. Family firms are in a unique and enviable position in that their cultures provide a link to strong beliefs and core values from the past. The role of the founder is crucial to establishing an organization's identity and purpose, and lingers on past his lifetime and into succeeding generations. This broader sense of self and focus on values frequently results in high-performance behaviors that lead to positive business outcomes. So the real question becomes: Is the organizational culture of a family business generally stronger than that of a non-family business? And, if so, why? How?

The Denison organizational culture model

To answer these questions we applied the Denison model developed by one of this chapter's authors over the past 15 years, with data from over 500 000 individuals. This model describes a theory of organizational culture that is linked to company performance. That is, the model and results generated by its Organizational Culture Survey equip senior decision-makers to fully leverage a company's existing strengths and identify potential weaknesses. This approach provides a useful tool for gaining insight and options for managers on the frontline of business decision-making.

The Denison model first gathers information from various levels of management on perceptions of their company's culture as manifested through its actions and activities. Then, data from respondents is described using a two-dimensional model highlighting the crucial issues of internal versus external focus and flexibility versus stability and their impact on performance and viability. These two dimensions can be viewed more as relative trade-offs rather than choices, as both an internal and an external focus are necessary for business success, as are both flexibility and stability.

An important goal of the model is to provide a mechanism for generalizing rather than highlighting uniqueness, in order to enhance comparability among organizations.

Utilizing these two important underlying dimensions, Denison supposed that while beliefs and assumptions lie at the core of corporate culture, they are expressed and identified via four cultural traits – Adaptability, Mission, Consistency, and Involvement. In turn, each of these traits is broken down further into three indices as shown in Figure 4.1. Associations between these four traits and indicators of corporate effectiveness, namely ROA,

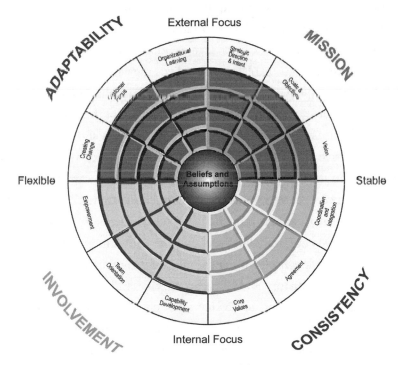

Figure 4.1 Denison organizational culture model

ROI, Sales Growth, Market Share, Quality, Employee Satisfaction, and Product/Service Development, were found to be significant.

Adaptability acknowledges an organization's struggle to continually balance internal and external events. Adaptability is measured by the three indices – Creating Change, Customer Focus, and Organizational Learning. A corporation's goals and vision for the future are expressed as Mission. A well-developed sense of purpose is measured by the following – Strategic Direction and Intent, Goals and Objectives, and Vision.

Consistency describes the unified approach to goal achievement and problem resolution that can provide internal resonance essential to dealing with outside challenges and unexpected situations. This trait is measured by – Core Values, Agreement, and Coordination and Integration. Finally, the empowerment and teamwork necessary to address the competitive environment can be expressed as Involvement. Indices measuring Involvement are as follows – Empowerment, Team Orientation, and Capability Development.

Through the survey, employees provide perceptions of their company's existing culture as measured according to the 12 indices. As shown in Figure 4.1, the more positive the corporation's culture, the more complete the circle. Once an organization identifies areas for improvement, it can pursue a course of action designed to correct vulnerabilities and accentuate cultural assets.

By using the method and model developed by Denison, we explored the relative advantages of family business culture, providing tangible proof that family enterprises are multi-dimensional, yet singular, organizations that claim a shared rich history and that can survive and prosper long after the personality-driven founder stage has passed. The focused, purposeful cultures found in many family businesses often go unrecognized as a source of competitive advantage. The aim, then, was to lend empirical credence to the concept of family business culture as distinctive, robust, and winning.

Testing the theory

Culture profiles for 47 family-owned firms were compared with those of 800 non-family firms. All data were collected between 1998 and 2003 and included a minimum number of respondents (10) per company. The organizations represented a cross-section of industries, geographies, ownership structures, and size. All organizations elected to take this survey and so both samples consisted of organizations that valued organizational culture. For the purposes of this study, family enterprises were defined as those firms that (a) had family voting ownership of 15% or more, or (b) had family members holding critical leadership positions, or family control of the company's governing body. The 47 family firms analyzed represented all the family firms in the Denison database.

Results

Family-owned firms had higher mean ratings on all 12 indices and, consequently, on all four traits. Family firms scored especially high on the agreement index, showing that family firms, on average, have substantially greater levels of internal congruence and a better chance of reaching consensus on important issues than non-family firms. (Refer to Table 4.1 for more detailed results.[1])

---

[1] For information on a similar, earlier study, please refer to: 'Culture in family-owned enterprises: recognizing and leveraging unique strengths' in the *Family Business Review*, March 2004 issue.

Table 4.1   Culture index and trait means for family-owned and non-family-owned businesses

Index or trait	Family-owned $n = 47$		Non-family-owned $n = 800$		Comparison	
	M	SD	M	SD	F	d[a]
Involvement	**3.48**	**0.25**	**3.41**	**0.28**	**2.22**	**0.22**
Empowerment	3.41	0.26	3.36	0.30	1.24	0.17
Team orientation	3.49	0.26	3.44	0.32	1.56	0.19
Capability development	3.52	0.26	3.44	0.27	3.65	0.29
Consistency	**3.35**	**0.23**	**3.29**	**0.26**	**2.42**	**0.23**
Core values	3.60	0.25	3.53	0.28	2.44	0.23
Agreement	3.33	0.22	3.23	0.26	6.02*	0.37
Coordination & integration	3.12	0.26	3.09	0.31	0.23	0.07
Adaptability	**3.33**	**0.19**	**3.28**	**0.23**	**2.58**	**0.24**
Creating change	3.20	0.25	3.14	0.28	2.16	0.22
Customer focus	3.55	0.24	3.49	0.27	2.15	0.22
Organizational learning	3.25	0.21	3.20	0.23	1.43	0.18
Mission	**3.34**	**0.26**	**3.29**	**0.29**	**1.54**	**0.19**
Strategic direction & intent	3.36	0.26	3.32	0.30	0.77	0.13
Goals & objectives	3.53	0.26	3.46	0.31	2.36	0.23
Vision	3.13	0.32	3.08	0.31	1.10	0.16

[a] d refers to a standardized mean difference, computed by dividing the difference between two means by their pooled standard deviation.
* $p < 0.05$.

As the table shows, respondents working at family-owned businesses provided higher mean ratings on all 12 indexes and all four traits. Differences between respondents from family-owned and non-family-owned businesses were not statistically significant, with the exception of the 'Agreement' index, $F(1,845) = 6.02$, $d = 0.37$. Differences in culture ratings were typically small in magnitude, with mean differences ranging in magnitude from 0.07 to 0.37 standard deviations. However, these differences were extremely consistent, with family-owned businesses scoring higher on all 12 dimensions of culture. A follow-up sign test indicated that this result was highly unlikely to have occurred due to chance, $z = 3.46$, $p < 0.001$.

What it means

For several generations, conventional management wisdom has supported the notion that widely held, listed corporations with clear separation of ownership and control were a superior organizational form compared to the family-owned firm. The results of this study clearly call that wisdom into question and demonstrate that there are cultural advantages associated with family-owned firms and that they have a distinct, performance-enhancing culture.

The most plausible explanation of these results involves the role of continuity of the founder's values in the company's culture. The distinct background and character of entrepreneurs led them to establish cultures that were not only rich in core values and performance-enhancing behaviors, but also to structure commercial environments more conducive to learning and encouraging of flexibility. Because these founder cultures are nurtured by succeeding generations of family who especially understood and maintained an emotional connection to the founder, culture in family-owned firms is difficult to replicate and so may be a source of strategic advantage. Gaining full benefit from cultural distinctiveness is a sober obligation to shareholders and the legacy of the founder.

Much conventional wisdom suggests that family firms are typically autocratic, inflexible, ambiguous in their direction, and resistant to investing in people. These views, from this data set, seem, on average, unfounded. Instead, family firms are apparently rife with cultural advantages.

It all starts with the founder

The strength and superiority of family business culture lies in its uniqueness. All companies begin life as the embodiment of a single individual's philosophies, hopes, fears and beliefs about relationships and the world. The founder is often a lone wolf, totally consumed with his ideas not only about what product or service to offer but with how to construct a world in which he feels comfortable and in full control. The fierce independence and need to define life on one's own terms typical of many business founders finds full bloom in entrepreneurship. The founder can recreate the world as it should have been in the first place and can thereby control his own destiny. Rather than living by the rules of others, entrepreneurs become entrepreneurs expressly to break out of prescribed molds and determine their own futures. They feel a need to stand up for what they believe in and for the world to take notice.

But asserting one's will in such a personal way means that entrepreneurs imbue their organizations with the full range of their individual idiosyncrasies. Their companies, through policies, procedures, and corporate behavior, may display contradictory beliefs or support conflicting notions, just like people. Family firms retain the founder culture, rather than falling prey to successive new generations of management wanting to emblazon their own seal on the non-family company. As the ultimate reflection of one human being, a founder's firm has a unique 'DNA.' Such a company's dynamics cannot easily be replicated. And perhaps, once a competitor succeeds in opening the cultural treasure trove, he finds little to emulate. No patterns, no blueprint – only what is. The firm's culture is as intangible as one's personality – it can be described but not copied. There is only one. So attempts at duplication are fruitless and meaningless to the prospective thief. A company, like an individual, can only finally be who they are. No amount of wishing for something different or more makes it so. Not all founders' companies manage to retain this innate value. A culture can be lost, homogenized or neutered through neglect or mismanagement. Harnessing the power of this competitive advantage, this secret weapon, is one of the family firm's greatest challenges – to 'know thyself' well enough to apply this knowledge efficiently in a competitive context.

This quirky uniqueness may hold the key to family enterprise success. Family business culture may be stronger, better, more long-lasting exactly because it remains the manifestation of a living, breathing imperfect person. Employees and successors can more authentically rally around this company, which is still the embodiment of the founder's core values as it is more real, more concrete, and has more meaning than the management proverb-of-the-month uttered by the endless succession of CEOs in non-family companies. Early management thinking concluded that people work for financial gain. But founders and employees are motivated by something more than money. Founders care about the business and profit but also about family, community, environment, history, and labor as people, and fashion their companies around these concerns. Employees, even generations later, can relate to the concept that while profit is important, so are other aspects of life and commerce. And, the primary stakeholders are not owners of equity, but rather customers and employees, on whom demand and supply ultimately rest. The founder and his family find peace with this idea, as it is perfectly in harmony with their view of the universe.

For many successful founders profit is necessary to survive but is not viewed as the sole or even primary reason to be in business. Family businesses typically have a legacy of being more connected to their community, employees, environment. Keeping the business going sustains these constituencies (Bartlett and Ghoshal, 2002). The wholeness of this approach contributes to a strong culture and ultimately the high performance observed in family companies. Ironically, business history has shown that companies that are not narrowly oriented around profit are generally more profitable. In the book *Built to Last*, the authors Jim Collins and Jerry Porras (1994) point to two enterprises, Merck & Company and Motorola, as examples of this phenomenon. George Merck firmly believed there was a moral imperative associated with the discoveries of science. Medicines should be developed for those in need and, as his son later echoed, 'the profits follow.' Motorola's purpose statement refers to the generation of profit as providing the opportunity for employment and personal accomplishment. Both corporations are hailed in the book as far surpassing their industry rivals, Pfizer and Zenith, respectively, in profitability.

By their very nature, founders are pragmatic. They are not theoretical relativists. They start businesses for a reason – to give shape to their personal ideas, beliefs, and preferences. In practice, they appear to have a foot in both worlds. They are down-to-earth realists who also dare to develop a personal view of corporate comportment that may not fit the conventional mold. In their own companies, forces like religious conviction or a code of living borne of childhood experience find a voice and means of expression. Collins and Porras call this the 'Genius of the AND.' They do not acknowledge a choice between consistency and flexibility or internal and external coherence. They choose both. This concept of 'AND' is one of the most potent features of family business culture uniqueness. Because of their singular history and the distinctive background of successors, family firms appear more adept at naturally balancing the 'AND.' Therein lies a key to stunning financial results and the general cohesive quality of family business culture.

A culture of maturity

Family companies that are not laser-focused on profit are more profitable – not the expected outcome. Firms with a unique heritage, a more holistic and universal outlook, inspire allegiance among employees. Hiring the right people in the first place is also crucial. But starting out with a solid set of authentic core values that serve as the touchstone for all corporate activities differentiates family companies. A stubborn dedication to the veracity of values goes a long way to providing an internal resonance that simply cannot be bought or purchased. There is no substitute for 'knowing thyself' in making strategic, organizational and competitive choices appropriate to the enterprise. Rather than the knee-jerk reaction of hiring an outside consultant to solve problems, responses to challenges developed internally are likely to be more resonant, more true to the corporation's real character. Does an outside expert know the company better than employees and management? Does the expert have the same chance of knowing what will work within the framework of the firm's shared philosophy? Some management theorists see a strong corporate culture as a negative factor limiting flexibility and creativity. But we suggest that rather than being a source of stodginess and rigidity, a company's internal resonance makes it a stronger, more coherent competitor, and, as such, one better equipped to face external challenges. A company with a strong sense of self can face the world with a confident and unified front. It is more agile because it has taken full stock of its capabilities and shortcomings but has over-arching confidence in its fundamental core values.

Maintenance required

Just because these cultures are 'natural' does not mean they are easy, require no upkeep, or lack rigor. Much thought, commitment and money must be invested in processes and procedures that support a healthy culture. This appears to run counter to expectations. If a culture is natural and represents a unique corporate 'DNA,' should not the answers to strategic or organizational issues come quickly and easily? But the truth is, mature cultures take more work and restraint than authoritative environments. It must be tempting at times for management to want to step in and impose a solution, rather than waiting for one to emerge from a contemplative, inclusive process. The best solution may not be fast or simple. But the one that emerges from an authentic, considered process is bound to be the most appropriate. A hallmark of such cultures is that they are mature, require maturity of participants, and respect the individual and the processes that keep the culture alive and working.

No substitute for painstaking recruitment

Excellence in hiring and other critical human resources practices is essential in a more evolved culture. Great care must be taken to choose employees who have independently developed a worldview in sync with the core values of the founder and family successors in the company. Attempting to convince an employee to buy into company philosophy for the sake of expediency does not work. In the face of personal or national beliefs that diverge from an employer's philosophy, what an individual truly believes will win out in determining action. Recruiting people who already share the family's and corporation's values means that management does not have to force or convert employees to their way of thinking and behaving.

Starting with a shared philosophy means less internal discord. The employee does not experience alienation from his true self and value system and so can be more committed to the success of the firm's goals. The common schism between management and staff does not exist in this scenario, as employees already possessing the requisite values sense a greater meaning to their work. Excellence may be achieved, not just for the sake of profit, but as a result of an enveloping, synchronous feeling of attachment to core values and ideals.

A positive environment in which the goals of the company and employees are aligned cannot help but result in a pleasant, fruitful work experience. In research conducted at the IMD-LODH Family Business Research Center, family-owned businesses were found to figure prominently in a list of 100 best places to work compiled by *Fortune* (Levering and Moskowitz, 2004). Further, 25% of the for-profit enterprises named for this honor were family firms, and two of the three finalists for the 2003 Bertelsmann Prize for corporate culture excellence were family businesses (the third was family-controlled until very recently). Creating a rewarding work environment makes supreme sense to successors, if for no other reason than it is the employees who are the foot soldiers in the sacred mission. Extending the founder's persona into perpetuity can only be accomplished through the dedicated effort of its staff. These believers, carriers of the corporate 'DNA,' make the founder's values come alive every day and prove the validity of his philosophy through action.

A successful culture like this is, in some sense, a non sequitur. The culture is supported by selecting people who already concur with existing core values. So adherence to the policies and procedures emanating from these values is a given, expected. However, once an individual is 'in' and accepted as a true believer, he or she is accorded full power to fashion the company's response to the business environment. He or she enjoys the freedom to act, innovate, make mistakes – once (Ghoshal and Bartlett, 1995). This personal resonance with the enterprise can have many mutual benefits, including prudent risk-taking and the ability to react to unforeseen circumstances. In this evolved culture, the employee does not have to guess how the boss or the organization will judge his or her response to an unanticipated situation – he or she already knows.

The critical role of successors

Successors are key in enabling the transfer of culture over time. The children of the founder often inherit the innate ability to balance apparent inconsistencies and competing aims. Learning to juggle multiple responsibilities and shuttle back and forth between tasks and roles is part of being a person. But founders' children have had the advantage of watching a role model who pursued an all-consuming business passion during the day and shared lessons, experiences and war stories at the dinner table. In their youth, Saturdays were spent at a miniature desk next to dad's. The line between work and life blurred. They watched the master as he simultaneously satisfied discrete constituencies and acknowledged divergent views, but ultimately discerned a singular path to his own authentic reality. Thus, successors learned early to see the trees despite the forest.

As they grow to maturity and gain positions of prominence in the family firm, founders' children or grandchildren do something that no one else is as uniquely qualified to do. As interpreters of family values in a business setting, they continue to mold the corporate culture in the image of the founder. The values that he carried through life were not only purposefully reflected in policies and procedures, office design and titling during his time at the firm. They were imparted to his children in a personal, informal manner that brought depth and greater understanding of the man himself. In the early entrepreneurial stage, the company functioned on the force of the founder's character and personality. Later, in his absence, successors act to give shape and form to the founder's ideas. With their enhanced insight, heirs codify an implicit understanding of the founder's philosophy for the next generation of managers and employees. The corporate culture becomes crisp, more accessible, more tangible.

Successors manage culture most effectively when they work diligently to understand the corporate culture and how to transmit it. This idea may seem surprising, given the company's rigorous staff selection process and that everyone on board is already in harmony with core values. So the 'natural' essence of the culture would seem to be something better left to flourish unimpeded. But active, invested management aimed at keeping the corporate culture attuned with its philosophical core pays dividends in internal synchronicity and superior performance.

Successors can also support cultural transmission by promoting stability during transition. The long tenure of most CEOs at family-owned enterprises allows the organizational dynamics planted by the founder to stabilize and take root. The American Family Business Survey (2003) found that the average term of a CEO at a family business could be as much as six times longer as at publicly held non-family counterparts. With consistent senior management, a company can build an institutional memory that guides the culture through strategic and competitive challenges. In non-family firms, changes in the CEO or chairman ranks are often accompanied by a full-scale clearing of the decks, complete with vilification of the former leadership. The upheaval and damaging instability, which often typify transfers of power in the executive suite generally, do not occur as frequently in family businesses. Family members acceding to company leadership positions are less likely to institute radical change for its own sake. The ego boost of imposing one's will, one's indelible imprint on an organization is anathema to healthy families. Basic core values are passed down in both a family and family business context, making such behavior unacceptable. The reality is 'the past is you.' To publicly and violently denigrate the past would be to trash dad or granddad. Simply not done.

So, successors are raised to balance competing aims and diverging forces. Yet, they are individuals in their own right, having an upbringing, life experience, education and personality different from the founder or their predecessor. But still, something remains the same, resonant with the past. Founders' children and grandchildren (or later heirs) maintain an allegiance to what they know to be true and yet bring the wealth of their own unique experience to managing the family business. The fact that their name is on the front door goes a long way toward motivating founders' heirs to continue the family legacy, albeit in their own manner. The role and challenges of successors illustrates the core truth of corporate adaptation – finding new ways to stay the same.

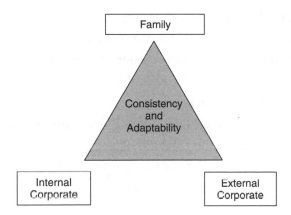

Figure 4.2   Family business dynamics

In the end, a triangle of consistency and adaptability emerges that renders a family business hard to beat and impervious to imitation, as illustrated in Figure 4.2.

Conclusion

- It is ironic that companies less focused on profit often demonstrate greater profitability.
- The founder as a unique, human person makes an indelible mark on the company throughout its lifetime.
- Greater focus on building organizational infrastructure can allow companies to last longer and do better.
- For a culture to be effective, it must result in better internal integration and better external adaptation.

- Choosing people in sync with company core values is key to the internal synchronicity successful cultures demonstrate.
- Successors support culture transmission through their innate knowledge of the founder's values and personality that, to varying degrees, they ultimately share in adulthood.
- The longer tenure of leadership in family firms sustains and strengthens the culture through stability and consistency.

References

American Family Business Survey. 2003. MassMutual Financial Group and Raymond Institute: 3.

Bartlett, C. and Ghoshal, S. 2002. 'Building competitive advantage through people.' *MIT Sloan Management Review*. Winter: 34–41.

Collins, J.C. and Porras, J.I. 1994. *Built to Last*. New York: HarperBusiness.

Fairlamb, D. 2003. 'The best European performers.' *Business Week*, 28 July: 50–55.

Ghoshal, S. and Bartlett, C.A. 1995. 'Changing the role of top management: beyond structure to process.' *Harvard Business Review*. January–February: 86–96.

James, H.S., Jr. 1999. 'Owner as manager, extended horizons and the family firm.' *International Journal of the Economics of Business*. Vol. 6, No. 1: 41–55.

Levering, R. and Moskowitz, M. 2004. 'The 100 best companies to work for.' *Fortune*, 12 January: 56–79.

Peters, T.J. and Waterman, R.H. 1982. *In Search of Excellence*. New York: Harper and Row.

Schein, E.H. 1985. *Organizational Culture and Leadership: A Dynamic View*. San Francisco: Jossey-Bass.

5
Understanding the Successor's Challenges

Joachim Schwass

A successor to the management of a family enterprise faces very special challenges. IMD research examining key elements in success or failure in succession situations found that obstacles are addressed in ineffective or incomplete ways and often lead to tension and frustration. As a result, the family, business, and individual suffer unnecessarily.

Most past emphasis on the development of next-generation leaders in family businesses has focused on their business competence. Typically, successors must prove themselves as managers and strategists. IMD studies indicate that successors are more accomplished as managers than is commonly believed. But they remain underdeveloped as individuals, as family leaders and as owners.

Underestimating the capabilities of successors is understandable. Popular wisdom holds that they are unlikely to be effective business leaders: they do not have the drive; they are selected more on the basis of who they are than by what they have accomplished; they often have impossibly large shoes to fill. Consequently, successors and those responsible for their development overreach in demonstrating the next generation's competence. This defensive posture exacerbates the successor's relative weaknesses in other dimensions necessary for long-term success – in the family, in the ownership group, and in personal fulfillment.

The objective of this chapter is to create a comprehensive, evolutionary framework for a successor and the family to understand and better prepare for challenges. The next chapter will further describe a workable, long-term talent development strategy, drawing on best practices from the world's leading family businesses.

The framework chosen for this chapter is built on the four key constituencies of the family business:

- Family
- Ownership
- Management
- Individual

Each of these groups has its own needs, interests, and driving forces. The proposed framework used to better understand these forces is evolutionary and changes as a family business successor moves through succeeding life cycle phases. The three distinct phases underlying this model are:

- The 'Do' phase
- The 'Lead to Do' phase
- The 'Let Do' phase

Considering the distinct phases of the successor's life cycle and how they are aligned with the forces driving the actions of the four constituencies (Family, Ownership, Management, Individual) allows us to frame the discussion in terms of the 'Successor's Phases Matrix.' This matrix is the basis for a comprehensive and rational appreciation for the complexity of one of the most crucial issues facing family firms. This chapter will conclude with an examination of the benefits of a less common approach to successor development.

The complexities of leadership succession in family businesses

Leadership succession is without doubt the most critical transition for any family business, irrespective of size, strategy, or performance. Leadership succession upsets an equilibrium that has become comfortable for the major constituencies of the family business system. The process begins as each generation defines its vision, thereby impacting strategy and the opportunity for individuals to play a role within the business. A common framework for all stakeholders emerges as the business leader seeks clarity on family expectations and intentions. It is generally in the interest of the business leader to maintain a well-defined and balanced approach to these groups in order to effectively manage strategic decision-making and expectations.

The arrival of a next-generation leader significantly impacts this equilibrium. The family is confronted with changes in the nature of existing relationships (from 'parent–child' to 'adult–adult'). Ownership is brought to the forefront as the next generation assumes the role of powerful leader. Management is impacted by the arrival of a new generation that possesses different levels of education and experience. And each individual – outgoing and incoming generations alike – is affected by the relentless march of time. The status quo established by the outgoing generation is challenged on all fronts as the heir apparent leader arrives.

Leadership succession in a family business is also considerably more complex than in non-family public corporations, mainly due to the following three factors:

- Family businesses are deeply influenced by the realities of concentrated ownership, both in terms of identity and proximity. Ownership is in the hands of a family and therefore not anonymous and not easily transferable. The family has a clearly defined identity and ownership objectives, generally standing in stark contrast to the short-term and more volatile goals of a non-family enterprise. In addition, the family is emotionally and financially close to the business. This familiarity brings both a broad and deep understanding of the company and an institutional memory, which is lacking in non-family firms.
- Leadership succession in a family business typically occurs between people related by blood, as from father to son. This family relationship adds an element of complexity, which brings both weakness and strength.
- The typical leadership tenure in a family business is long. The tenure ranges from a decade to 30 or 40 years. In larger non-family corporations, research points to dramatically shorter periods.

What does this mean for the successor?

The strong linkage of family and business over an extended time horizon has unique implications for the successor in a family business. First and foremost, the legacy of the outgoing leader leaves an indelible imprint on the business. The sole reference point for 'the way things are done around here' is one person, often the founder, who has led the business through good times and bad. Serious implications for the successor follow, as navigating a culture that is the embodiment of his predecessor, frequently his father, can be treacherous. The successor's familiarity with the business and decision-making process can offset these dangers, however.

Alternatively, any changes undertaken by the successor will be viewed as a criticism of previous decisions. The potential for inter-generational conflict is enormous. And a corporate overhaul, particularly from the perspective of a successor who arrives with a shiny new MBA, may be seen as long overdue. Indeed, an extended leadership tenure risks focusing too much on historically proven products and processes at the expense of prudent risk-taking and innovation. Often, the next-generation successor perceives a strategy too oriented toward the past.

In summary, a successor faces many serious issues:

- A business culture defined by one individual;
- A business strategy based on past experiences;
- A complex, evolving parent–child relationship.

These issues typically lead to conflict among the generations and other stakeholders. IMD experience has shown that the vast majority of family businesses are inadequately prepared to address potential stumbling blocks. Research data from several countries confirms that less than one quarter of family businesses have an explicit, written succession plan. The lack of a comprehensive plan to prepare for leadership succession and its unavoidable impact considerably increases the risk of failure.

Risk of failure

The costs of ineffectively handling this important process can be enormous and even result in total failure of the business. One very visible and highly publicized example is the Swiss-based André Trading Group, which went bankrupt (Vermot, 2001). The André Group, known as one of the 'Five Sisters' of world grain trading, was founded in 1877 to import grain and other food products. It was under the leadership of third-generation Georges André that the business experienced impressive growth, mainly through global grain, cocoa, coffee, and rice trading. In the 1980s the company operated in 70 countries and generated revenues said to exceed $10 billion. But in the 1990s, things started to change as the transparency of the Internet brought direct market access and diminished the role of the traditional trader.

The André family had always been intensely private and reluctant to share detailed financial results. Fourth-generation Henri André eventually assumed the title of chairman. However, his predecessor, Georges, maintained effective control well into the 1990s. Henri, who had wanted to become an architect, had accepted the role as chairman in allegiance to the family. Complicated emotional entanglements paralyzed Henri and diverted his attention from implementing difficult but necessary change. Following a period of rapid deterioration and heavy losses, in March 2001 the company filed for protection from its creditors. The local press blamed the failure on inadequate succession planning.

The real challenges for successors?

When trying to identify reasons for family business failure following a succession, comments like, 'The son did not have his father's knack for business,' are often heard.

The failure is naturally attributed to the successor, as the unthinkable happened on his watch. But the lack of leadership skills blamed on the successor normally only represents the tip of the iceberg. The true cause is much deeper and more complex. Henri André shed further light on this:

> I could not address some of the real and fundamental problems of the business because this would have meant overturning key decisions taken by the previous leaders to whom I am particularly close: my father and my uncle. For my father, restructuring would have meant abandoning everything that he and his father had built up. (Grand and Roberts, 2001)

This insight from the leader of a failed family business implies that the need for change was there and understood, but family relationships prevented the necessary from being done. Emotional complications restricted the actions of the next generation in introducing needed change. This is where the fundamental differences between family and non-family corporations emerge. A successor in a non-family company puts the past firmly behind him and may even question the competence and credibility of his predecessor. This has, more often than not, become the case in non-family firms. Discrediting the previous regime allows the new leader to start with a clean slate. General rules of thumb for successors in corporations with widely disbursed ownership include focusing on the future and breaking with the past by overturning decisions made by the predecessor.

The world's most visible and consistently profitable firm, General Electric (GE), is an example of these concepts. In 1981 the outgoing CEO, Reginald Jones, advised his successor on the best approach for the future, 'Blow it up.' The name of the successor was Jack Welch. Welch changed the fundamental strategies of his predecessor and led GE to outstanding success, primarily through acquisition. Twenty years later, Jack Welch, in turn, advised his successor, Jeffery Immelt, to 'Blow it up.' Since ascending to the GE throne, Immelt has actively overturned the acquisitions-based strategy of his much-lauded predecessor by preaching the virtues of internal growth (Useem, 2004).

GE's experience illustrates the typical successor's paradigm – assert yourself quickly through the development of new strategies. While this philosophy is visibly applied in corporations seeking to meet ever-higher stakeholder performance requirements, successors in family businesses have also adopted this approach, though for vastly different reasons. The need for recognition and acceptance as a competent leader by the predecessor, usually the father, drives the next-generation family business leader to act quickly and boldly. The unique organizational and governance dynamics found in family firms are driven by the confluence of the four above-mentioned constituencies found only in family businesses – Family, Owner-ship, Management and the Individual.

In non-family corporations, the business is steered by management as ownership is widely dispersed. In a family business, it is the family that is at the core of ownership and in turn directs its overall strategy, culture and goals. The next-generation successor is subjected to the constraints set by these interested parties. For leadership to be successful, a balanced approach to recognizing and understanding how these distinct groups interact is essential. Effective family business leadership attempts to create equilibrium between the, at times, overlapping and competing aims of its stakeholders.

The potential for conflict is high and increases as succession becomes imminent. Over the lifetime of the successor, this equilibrium needs to be modified in response to constant internal and external change.

Understanding the successor's challenges and their evolution through the 'Successor's Phases Model'

The characteristics of and interaction among the four constituencies evolve over time. Time is an important component in this analysis, as individuals evolve through a series of lifelong changes. In family businesses, the moniker 'successor' tends to be applied for a considerably longer time period than in a widely held corporation. The reasons for this lie in the continuity of ownership and the collective memory of the family. Management and staff also tend to differentiate successors from the earlier generation. So while the label 'successor' often stays for decades, the underlying responsibilities evolve, and along with them, the needs and interests of the successor.

Three main leadership phases from the perspective of the professional life cycle of a successor can be summarized as:

- Do
- Lead to Do.
- Let Do

The 'Do' phase begins when a successor joins the family business. Typically this person assumes a less responsible position but with the clear purpose of learning and understanding the business. The 'Lead to Do' phase starts with the promotion to a leadership role with clearly defined authority. Finally, the 'Let Do' phase covers the retirement of the successor, overlapping with the 'Do' phase of the next generation.

Successors entering the family business usually do not think of succession as a lengthy apprenticeship. Rather, they focus on the 'Lead to Do' phase. Due to the generally long tenure of family business leaders, the next generation has not observed their parent's journey through the 'Do' phase. They therefore expect the perks of the 'Lead to Do' phase but not the hard slog which precedes them. It is in the 'Do' phase that understanding takes place which ultimately qualifies the successor for leadership. The next chapter will discuss this more fully.

The next section considers the successor's leadership hurdles both in terms of the three sequential phases and the four different constituencies.

The 'Do' phase

This phase begins with employment at an entry level. The challenges the successor faces within this phase can be analyzed as follows.

Family

Family influence typically remains strong during the 'Do' phase, as the successor tends to be relatively young, between 25 and 35 years. Family influence is also felt as active communication between generations regarding the ascendancy of the offspring commences. The most problematic challenge lies in the changing relationship dynamics between the generations. Both struggle, as the senior generation tends to favor the continuation of the traditional hierarchical relationship, while the successor attempts to make forward progress. In periods of inter-generational conflict, the parent–child relationship tends to prevail and lead to deteriorating communications.

Ownership

During the 'Do' phase, the ownership challenge relates to uncertainty. The parent generation typically sees no point in anticipating the future transfer of ownership, preferring to keep their options open. They often harbor concerns about the competence and commitment of the next generation. In other cases, the parents may want to delay naming a successor to see which of their children ultimately holds the most promise. They may be unsure how to effectively pass on ownership if not all of their offspring are involved in the business. Or they may simply perceive ownership as a vehicle for controlling the business and family. The next generation initially waits, trusting the parents to address the issue fairly.

Management

During the 'Do' phase the trials for the successor revolve around finding the appropriate balance between personal aspirations and professional competence. The objective is to gain approval and recognition as a skilled manager, while

Interests Phase	Family	Ownership	Management	Individual
'Do'	Child–parent relationship	Control dependent	Professional assertion	Personal leadership

Figure 5.1   The 'Do' phase

still learning the ropes. Successors know they are under particularly close observation. This feeling of being in a 'fish-bowl' can place severe strain on the wellbeing of the successor.

Individual

Learning, testing and uncertainty characterize the 'Do' phase from this perspective. The focus centers on rapidly reaching a platform of independence from the family and recognition within the business. Personal financial and psychological safety concerns dog the successor, whose primary challenge involves developing *personal* leadership. The 'Do' phase can therefore be summarized as in Figure 5.1.

The 'Lead to Do' phase

The 'Lead to Do' phase kicks in when the successor is promoted to greater levels of responsibility, usually around 35–50 years of age. The challenges faced by the successor in this phase are analyzed relative to the four major stakeholders.

Family

In the 'Lead to Do' phase, the traditional familial relationship undergoes fundamental change, as the next generation gains both personal and professional independence. Another key factor is the creation of a new nuclear family with marriage and children bringing new realities and maturity for the successor. As emotional distance increases, the separation process may be painful to the parents, yet seem natural to the adult child. The parent–child relationship shifts to an adult peer relationship. This transition is often abetted by business power struggles. The 'Lead to Do' phase is characterized by a growing distance between the generations that greatly increases the potential for conflict and challenges for the successor.

Ownership

The 'Lead to Do' phase is marked by a struggle for ownership control. The parents, experiencing a loss of influence over the next generation in both the family and business realms, view ownership as the last vestige of control. Frequently, the successor considers the alternative of staying versus leaving the family business, feeling unfairly treated by the parents. If there are siblings involved who are not active in the business, the successor feels the need for clarity on ownership distribution. Both sides engage in a contentious struggle for control of the family and business.

Management

In the 'Lead to Do' phase, the successor has typically achieved a more viable alignment between personal aspirations, professional competence and business needs. A strong track record leads to a higher confidence and recognition level for the successor. The major challenge shifts to establishing boundaries between the influence of the outgoing and incoming leader. Both the successor and management are confronted with an ambiguous situation, as the new leadership powers of the successor can be usurped by the senior generation.

The 'Lead to Do' phase sees a building of a power base by the successor and attempts to replace existing management with a new loyal team. This is a particularly difficult time for the business, as it becomes the battleground of the generations.

Individual

The 'Lead to Do' phase is distinct in that the learning period gives way to a time of stabilization and consolidation. The horizon shifts to medium term as the vision for the business is clearer, but the lack of ownership control is perceived as a complicating factor. Personal and professional recognition and self-esteem are primary objectives, and status plays an important role.

The successor's mindset in the 'Lead to Do' phase now broadens to recognize the needs of others. This finds expression in the business as team-based management becomes the norm and developing *organizational* leadership becomes more urgent. The needs of the nuclear family receive new-found attention.

Interests Phase	Family	Ownership	Management	Individual
'Lead to Do'	Adult–adult relationship	Control struggle	Leadership assertion	Organizational leadership

Figure 5.2 The 'Lead to Do' phase

The successor's challenges in the 'Lead to Do' phase can be summarized as in Figure 5.2.

The 'Let Do' phase

Around the age of 50–65, the successor may still see the parent generation alive and wielding moral influence on the family business.

Family

The successor begins to see his own children as next generation successors. The important challenge is the development of a positive inter-generational relationship, which integrates lessons learned – both negative and positive – from the successor's own experience. IMD research shows that inter-generational attachments tend to suffer irreparable damage following a negative encounter. Thus, if a successor had suffered from parental interference, he will assume a more detached posture with his own children. The reverse can also apply.

Ownership

In the 'Let Do' phase, ownership takes on new meaning now that control has been achieved. Predecessors may cling to ownership as a guarantor of power over the next generation. More positively, ownership may be intellectually dissociated from individual family members and be perceived as a vehicle to create wealth for a growing family. The challenge, particularly in the 'Let Do' phase, is to implement this vision without regard to one's own personal power, and establish policies and initiatives supportive of the family's long-term needs.

Management

The senior generation may be struggling to retain operational influence. However, as the next generation assumes leadership, the business is typically focused on innovation and adaptation. The older generation tends to compensate for this loss of day-to-day power by asserting greater influence on corporate governance issues.

Individual

The 'Let Do' phase brings fundamental challenge and change to the successor who now faces the next successor's rise to power. The main hurdle is to define a new meaning to life distinct from leadership activities. This immensely difficult challenge requires humility, the adoption of a long-term time horizon and genuine concern for future generations. Motivational

Phase \ Interests	Family	Ownership	Management	Individual
'Let Do'	Parent–child relationship	Control versus vision	Governance assertion	Institutional leadership

Figure 5.3   The 'Let Do' phase

needs shift from solely addressing self-esteem to a greater emphasis on personal fulfillment. In other words, the successor measures his achievements by his ability to create opportunities for family. The mindset increasingly shifts to the needs of others and in developing *institutional* leadership. Therefore, the 'Let Do' phase can be summarized as in Figure 5.3.

The 'Successor's Phases Matrix'

The successor's challenges are summarized in Figure 5.4.[1]

Conclusion

The complexity and potential risk of failure of succession in a family enterprise are significant. In IMD's experience, in most cases the successor lacks

---

[1] The Successor's Phases Matrix is excerpted from the author's forthcoming book, *Wise Growth Strategies in Leading Family Businesses*, London: Palgrave, 2005.

Phase \ Interests	Family	Ownership	Management	Individual
'Do'	Child–parent relationship	Control dependent	Professional assertion	Personal leadership
'Lead to Do'	Adult–adult relationship	Control struggle	Leadership assertion	Organizational leadership
'Let Do'	Parent–child relationship	Control versus vision	Governance assertion	Institutional leadership

Figure 5.4   The Successor's Phases Matrix

a comprehensive and systematic understanding of imminent obstacles. Too much emphasis may be placed on preparing for the transition and not enough on evolutionary shifts over the life cycle of the firm.

The success of a transition may be enhanced through an appreciation of and better planning for the ongoing complexity of the succession process. Three key takeaways emerge from our research at IMD.

Successors jump the gun

Upon entering the family business, heirs tend to assume a posture appropriate to the 'Lead to Do' phase, omitting the learning and development experience that should have preceded it.

Successors focus too narrowly

Successors attempt to gain validation from rapidly asserting their new-found power at the expense of the needs of the family and prudent business governance. Successors often are so consumed with their own needs that they are oblivious to the big picture.

Successors lack empathy for other stakeholders

Since successors tend to be impatient with the leadership development process and focus narrowly on management needs, they tend to be too egocentric. They lack empathy for other stakeholders in the family business system who have legitimate interests and needs.

The model introduced here provides an opportunity for the successor to understand and plan the most effective way to address a complex situation. In addition, each successor will gain better insight into the next generation's dilemmas. More in-depth consideration of these issues should encourage greater empathy and a superior family business leadership successor development strategy.

References

Grand, J. and Roberts, A. 2001. 'Swiss grain trader counts the cost of family ties: the restructuring of André has failed.' *Financial Times*, 4 April: 38

Useem, J. 2004. 'Another boss, another revolution.' *Fortune*, 5 April: 112–121.

Vermot, P. 2001. 'André & Cie. Pousse son chant du cygne et met fin à ses activités commerciales.' *Agefi*, 12 March: 8.

6

An Effective Successor Development Strategy

Joachim Schwass

In the previous chapter, the challenges of the four constituencies of a family business were considered. A model was presented that explored the evolution of the firm and the successor life cycle. The discussion concluded that the typical approach to succession, focusing on management and strategy, is incomplete and ineffective because:

- Successors jump the gun;
- Successors focus too narrowly;
- Successors lack empathy for other stakeholders.

This chapter builds on the insights gained from the previous description of the successor's challenges and proposes a strategy for successor development that emphasizes both the importance of the linkages among the four constituencies and successor development as a phased process. The successor needs to understand that in a family business, it is the family that determines the ownership strategy, which subsequently influences management. Focusing on management strategy first and foremost underestimates the importance of addressing both family and ownership needs. By involving family at an early stage, the successor increases the chance of a more balanced, less disruptive start in the family business. The successor must take the initiative and personal responsibility for the development plan and must reach out to family members and especially the predecessor. Successors often feel reluctant to engage the senior generation and believe family leaders should more appropriately reach out to them. While that assumption seems reasonable in many respects, following that path precludes a valuable opportunity for the successor to show leadership and empathy for the interests of others. In the long run, respect and support by the other family owners determines the success of the successor.

The active inclusion of the parent generation needs first to overcome two major hurdles. At the early stages of the process, both generations tend to adopt communication styles that are incompatible with achieving a mutually satisfactory outcome. The successor development strategy proposed in this chapter overcomes these difficulties through a comprehensive three-dimensional growth plan. It is logical for successors to take the initiative since this action will undoubtedly demonstrate leadership ability, and because they are the ones who will be most critically affected by the results of this strategy.

About inter-generational communication

The successor strategy recognizes the difficulties in inter-generational communication typically found at the early stages of a succession. IMD research has clearly indicated that, without guidance and consideration of the issues raised through the model, interaction between the outgoing and the incoming generations is generally unproductive. Several factors highlight the difficulties.

Lack of experience

Succession is a rare event for everyone involved. The infrequent occurrence of succession infuses the situation with a heightened level of insecurity. Further, past experience of a succession does not necessarily help in providing meaningful guidelines for the next transition. This is particularly relevant when a cultural shift transpires due to significant family expansion in the next generation. Attempting to force an 'I' culture, marked by a single dominant owner-manager, on an 'US' culture, made up of a team of next-generation siblings, is simply counterproductive. The same can be said for the transition from an 'US' to an 'US and THEM' culture which occurs when family size causes a wide dispersion of member interests and needs. Each succession has its own characteristics and requirements that are fundamentally determined by present and, more importantly, future needs.

Confusing hats

The arrival of a next generation in the family business brings a period of uncertainty for all. Enhanced communication helps ease this situation but requires an extremely focused approach, as ownership and management roles now complicate the content of the message. Negative information transmitted from the senior to the younger generation, in particular, tends to create additional strains on the relationship.

Unchanging communication style

How generations communicate is also greatly altered. The traditional parent–child style needs to be brought in alignment with an acknowledgment that communication will shift to a more business-oriented interaction. Family members are typically not good communicators among themselves because early patterns of communication tend to persist. As the relationship between the generations evolves, communication styles tend to lag in adapting to the needs of a more business-oriented and factual exchange of information. Further increasing the potential for conflict is the fact that the quality and manner of communication tends to fluctuate, resulting in confusion and mixed messages.

What do they want?

The inherent difficulties in handling succession are further exacerbated by the parties' preconceptions. IMD research has clearly concluded that both generations approach the issues around succession with highly ineffective mindsets.

For several years, during IMD's Leading the Family Business program, one key assignment sought to cut through this quagmire. Participants were separated into two groups, outgoing generation and incoming generation, and were asked to list their recommendations for better facilitating succession to the other. For many participants, this was the first time they took the time to acknowledge the needs of others. In addition, considering the question in a peer group enhances the breadth and depth of the discussion. Figures 6.1 and 6.2 list the most frequently cited recommendations.

- Obtain a top-notch education
- Gain outside experience
- Start at the bottom
- Learn about all facets of the business
- Choose the best employees, including those more accomplished than yourself
- Understand your obligation toward your family
- Be proud of your family
- Don't expect us to make decisions for you

Figure 6.1   Typical advice from the older generation to potential successors

- Plan early for transition
- Find other activities to fill your time
- Focus on tax and financial planning
- Clear up unresolved issues
- Plan how to introduce new family members
- Give shares early
- Create business and family governance structures
- Be clear about your intentions/wishes/interests
- Accept that change is necessary
- Assure your own economic independence
- Be open to the idea of an outside facilitator
- Let go!

Figure 6.2   Typical advice from the rising generation to their elders

Insights

These comments have varied little over the years and reveal a surprising consistency and overlap between the generations. The parent–child relationship is clearly at work. Parents tell the next generation what to do with great authority, while the younger generation requests clarity and preparation. Both reflect typical parent–child behavioral roles.

There is consistency too in the players' mindsets, as each generation expects the other to undertake initiatives for the benefit of the other. This research suggests that neither generation adopts a very constructive, selfless approach. The apparent lack of empathy between relatives needs to be resolved for the good of the family and business.

The change initiative

During succession, the inter-generational relationship fluctuates between an authoritarian interaction and a more future-oriented peer style. This is particularly true in direct successions from parents to children. Volatility in these key relationships causes insecurity and anxiety, particularly for the incoming generation whose objective is to realize personal and professional validity. The younger generation clearly has the most to gain from pressing for a rapid evolution in the fundamental relationship. However, a profound cultural shift will be necessary to disrupt the hierarchical parent–child relationship. A 'bottom up' initiative by the next generation is generally perceived as an act of protest and revolution against an established order and system. The most frequent resolution involves an extended period of trial and error, during which the next generation tests out new boundaries that are often rebuffed by the parents. The fundamental nature of this inter-generational exchange is that of opponents: 'You versus Me.' This implies a 'lose–win' situation that damages family harmony.

A culture of trust and respect sustains family unity and is easier to achieve within a 'win–win' scenario. For both generations to win, they must create and share a vision of the culture that benefits both generations. Most successful family businesses embrace 'bottom up' initiatives by the next generation which desires change and will clearly gain the most from a smooth transition.

The growth-based 'I' initiative

Since the objective of the 'I' initiative by the successor is to introduce change that benefits both generations, the interests of all four stakeholders must be addressed. Growth stands out as a consistent, unifying theme. In order to prevail, it is necessary to recognize the key objectives of the four constituencies described in Chapter 5, found in successful, long-lasting family businesses. IMD research has identified the objectives listed in Table 6.1.

A growth-based 'I' initiative by the successor effectively targets the needs of all parties. The development strategy addresses these needs in an evolutionary way, as expressed by the successor's desire to:

- Grow as an individual;
- Grow as a leader of the business;
- Grow the business.

Successors gain multiple benefits from this three-dimensional development strategy since it demonstrates that they see succession as a gradual process. Such a demonstration of humility to family and other stakeholders creates a climate of confidence and trust that attracts support integral in helping successors grow into their role over time. The unconventional aspect of this successor development process is that it is actively and transparently initiated

Table 6.1   Key objectives of the four constituencies

Constituency	Objective
Family	Harmony by providing personal growth opportunities to all
Ownership	Wealth preservation and growth
Management	Business growth
Individual	Sense of purpose through personal growth

by the successor. Transparency, coupled with humility and the willingness to first grow as an individual, are key components in ensuring that this strategy is viewed as meaningful and worthy of family support. This successor development strategy ideally addresses the needs of all involved and the transparent and systematic process ensures broadly based support.

The following sections illustrate various elements of this growth strategy, based on best practices of successful multi-generational family businesses.

Growing as an individual

The first dimension of the successor development strategy is the successors' recognition that they must grow as people. The importance of individual growth is probably best reflected in the following statement made by Pietro Barilla, third-generation chairman of the Barilla Group, as he faced retirement:

> As family members leading a family business we must offer something
> of ourselves – the best of what we are.

At the beginning, each successor aspiring to a leadership role in the family business needs to internalize the commitment to develop and grow as an individual in order to achieve the respect of others. It is important for the successor to undertake this initiative proactively, rather than respond to pressure from others.

There appear to be two types of successors. The first type possesses an inherent sense of curiosity that ignites a desire to continually seek new experiences. The second type has not yet expressed an interest in growing. Research on successor development in family businesses indicates that this can best be triggered through interactions with older visionary leaders. Many successors appear to be deeply inspired by earlier generations of family business leaders. The fourth-generation successor team of the Zegna Group openly expresses its admiration for leaders from previous generations, and most particularly for Ermenegildo Zegna who, in the second generation, laid the crucial foundation for the firm's strong growth. What is important is that the desire for personal growth can be nurtured over time.

Which leadership qualities best serve as a guideline toward achieving personal growth? Interviews with senior business leaders produced the results shown in Figure 6.3.

- Knowledgeable
- Experienced
- Logical
- Decisive
- Courageous
- Creative
- Intuitive
- Energetic
- Engaging
- Optimistic
- Devoted

Figure 6.3   Leadership qualities for personal growth

Not all leaders possess all of these qualities and successful leaders also exhibit different qualities. However, two qualities on the list, knowledge and experience, are necessary for a developing successor candidate. Successors need to be inspired by examples of these leadership qualities in others.

What is the most effective way for a successor to grow through knowledge and experience? This varies from person to person. But research and modern learning theory (Hill, 2001) indicate that a well-structured process greatly enhances knowledge and experience in a successor.

In the past, learning was seen as an informational process that consisted of acquiring and storing knowledge. In the 1980s, new research emerged that challenged this assumption. Learning was seen as a transformational process that modified the learner's general worldview and basic assumptions. The human was viewed not as a machine that stored information but rather a being that experienced emotion. D.A. Kolb (1984) introduced four steps in this transformational learning process (see Figure 6.4).

Learning first involves a concrete experience, followed by reflective observation or an information-gathering phase, abstract conceptualization leading to an analytical model to make sense of the experience, and finally active experimentation allowing a structured and systematic transformation.

This model is particularly relevant for a successor who wants to grow as a person, since it stresses the importance of experience in the learning cycle.

- Concrete experience
- Reflective observation
- Abstract conceptualization
- Active experimentation

Figure 6.4   Kolb's learning model

Increasing numbers of experiences, especially if analyzed and conceptualized, can lead to better knowledge and in turn a stronger leader. Research shows that most family firms restrict the successor's experiences to their own business. By doing so, the growth benefits are narrowed and learning opportunities are limited, as is the successor's ability to demonstrate new-found competencies. These dynamics result in a vicious cycle, where limited experiences lead to limited understanding and limited potential application in the family business. Best practices from leading family businesses point toward a three-phased approach that more effectively enhances the growth of the successor.

Phase one: The learning steps are limited to developing as an individual within the context of the family business. While this makes it difficult for the successor to actively experiment, the benefits lie in gaining a deeper understanding of the family business. Concrete experiences are created by early employment in the family enterprise. Some families, however, prefer that the members of the next generation keep their distance from the family firm in their formative years. Meaningful learning comes instead from interaction with senior-generation family members. Many multi-generational family businesses create both formal and informal opportunities for inter-generational learning. This can take place during family reunions and celebrations where time is provided for the young to ask questions. In some cases, successors interview older family members about their experiences and write an article or book on the family's history. Understanding the history of the family business is highly prized by the older generation and can be a valuable initiative to undertake. Most successful multi-generational family businesses exhibit highly effective strategic linkages between tradition and innovation. Past practices and strategies provide an important education to the successor, as business innovation strategies are contemplated. The successor's deep understanding of the history of the family business is absolutely essential. Interviews with current and former employees and other stakeholders can provide valuable outside perspectives.

One highly effective form of learning is group attendance at a family business seminar. Participants generally emerge from such an experience more committed and united in their purpose.

In phase one, the strongest individual growth opportunities are based on learning from others connected to the family business. Structured learning events can potentially increase the depth and breadth of the learning and a focused commitment to education. Language studies are seen as a vehicle to expand learning, and higher-level studies in disciplines related to the family business are common.

Phase two: The learning process now takes place outside the business and away from the family. Through concrete work and life experiences in new and different environments, the individual capacity toward abstract conceptualization is greatly enriched. One's own family and business are no longer the only game in town and meaningful new learning can take place. Professional work experience in other companies also leads to experimentation opportunities, which are harder to achieve in the family business. In many of the world's successful family businesses, the successor saw outside experience as an opportunity to escape from overpowering senior-generation family leaders and thereby develop a greater sense of independence. Guido Barilla, fourth-generation chairman of the Barilla Group, has commented that he moved to New York early in his career in order to be independent of his father. Similarly, fourth-generation Gildo Zegna of the Zegna Group started his working career as a buyer at Bloomingdales in New York.

Phase three: The learning process now takes place within the family business as the successor enters the leadership track. Having returned with enhanced knowledge and experience gained outside, the successor now finds it increasingly possible to experience the full learning cycle – including active experimentation. This strengthens both the level of self-confidence and respect from others. Many successors who saw benefits in distancing themselves from the family during phase two, actively seek learning and development opportunities outside the family business, even as they return to their roots and assume a management post. Associations such as the Young Presidents' Organization and the Family Business Network provide opportunities to meet with peers from other family businesses and from different parts of the world. This enables personal benchmarking which can stimulate the desire for ongoing individual growth. These and other organizations offer focused educational programs and learning activities addressing the needs of successors. Growing as an individual ideally becomes a lifelong mission.

Personal growth first requires a willingness to grow and can often be acquired through the inspiration of respected leaders. But the most meaningful learning can come from a deep understanding of the family's business history. Individual growth is a process of learning and experience. Structuring this process in three phases – inside the family business, then outside and finally inside again – provides opportunities that are of particular relevance and benefit to family business successors. Ongoing contacts with peers serve as valuable personal benchmarking mechanisms underpinning the motivation for continuous growth.

Growing as a leader of the business

Growing in the role of business leader can best be facilitated if it is understood as a managed process. Three important lessons have been culled from the experience of leading family businesses. First, successors must submit themselves to a career development plan. Second, the successors must systematically develop their own vision for the future of the family and business relationship. Third, the leadership transition from the outgoing generation to the successors should be staged as a formal celebration.

A second-generation successor who started to work in his family business expressed his experience about growing in the role of family business leader as follows:

> I had not realized the extent to which I had to submit myself to different company rules. Non-family employees were highly suspicious of me and learning on the job proved to be very difficult.

Successors deciding to work in the family firm should follow a detailed career development plan that provides for independent assessment of strengths and weaknesses and leads to a progress plan according to performance-based milestones. This can reduce criticism from both family and non-family members that the successor's appointment was not based solely on merit. A career plan is particularly important when the successor is young and has little outside experience. Multi-year experience gained independent of the family company helps shape character, understanding and self-confidence. The advice of human resources professionals from inside and outside the family business throughout the successor's career is crucial in developing the requisite leadership skills.

When fourth-generation Sam Johnson entered his family business, S.C. Johnson & Sons in the USA, his father hired a consulting firm to design a career plan for Sam. Although initially resistant, Sam was presented with internal learning assignments that prepared him for his appointment as head of the new product development department.

Later on in life, Sam affirmed the wisdom and benefits of this professionally developed process, noting that it helped build the trust and confidence of people around him.

'Visioning' is another key element in growing in the role of leader. With the support of the older generation, the successor develops and formulates a future vision for the family business. This is a formal process that obliges the successor to re-examine the linkages that hold the family and business together. The key question is: What is the role of the next generation as owners and managers of the family enterprise? This process should be guided by outside consultants and will undoubtedly take place gradually. Once the next generation has shaped a comprehensive vision, a symbolic end to the parent–child relationship occurs. The visioning process should make allowances for the empathetic and constructive retirement of the outgoing generation. Best practices drawn from successful multi-generational family businesses indicate that the senior generation can significantly contribute to the ongoing professionalism and effectiveness of the governance process. Third-generation Mariano Puig Sr., chairman of the Puig Corporation in Spain, commented:

> My role is to ensure that the right questions are being asked, but not to give answers; that my successors should do.

Finally, passing the baton from one generation to the next is an important milestone for those who are directly concerned. But stakeholders inside and outside the business may also feel uncertainty about future changes. This is a moment of great emotional turmoil for those leaving the top position. When the transition to third-generation leadership of Puig took place, a major celebration commemorated the event. Over 120 key managers, clients and suppliers were invited to join the family as the outgoing generation formally presented a history of the company. The successors then discussed its plans for the future. The formality of this event clarified the beginning of a new leadership era to all stakeholders and the achievements of previous leaders were appropriately recognized.

Growing as a leader of the business is most effectively undertaken within the context of a structured process, including a career development plan implemented and monitored by human resources specialists, development of a vision for the family business by heirs, and formal recognition that a new era of leadership is underway. A well-considered process for growing leaders into their roles can enhance credibility and trust.

Growing the business

The vast majority of smaller and medium-sized family businesses grow very little. A growth-oriented approach is critical, particularly for families with broad-based ownership: a growing number of family owners means an increasing roster of those receiving dividend checks. Market conditions change, and adaptation and renewal are essential. Growth built on a vision developed and formulated in turn by each generation confirms a sense of personal worth and professional achievement. Instead of just inheriting a business and a vision, the successor generation contributes in their own right.

Best practices from the most successful family companies indicate that business growth should be wise and considered. Particularly for family businesses that are mindful of their tradition, evolutionary growth is generally more effective than revolutionary change. An example of intelligent growth is Ermenegildo Zegna. The growth strategy of each successive generation maintained the earlier generation's achievements and enhanced them with distinctive strategies (see Figure 6.5).

The Zegna Group is an excellent example of intelligent growth accomplished through a forward vertical integration strategy. Other business growth strategies are equally applicable and relevant for family businesses (see Figure 6.6).

Wise growth effectively links tradition with innovation. Understanding tradition is a key task for a successor and requires formal and informal interaction with the older generation. A growth strategy requires courage, the willingness to take calculated risks, and a healthy sense of self-confidence

Generation 1: Spinning   –   –   –

Generation 2: Spinning + weaving

Generation 3: Spinning + weaving + confection   –

Generation 4: Spinning + weaving + confection + retail

Figure 6.5   Zegna: generational business growth strategies

- Internationalization
- Diversification to related products
- Diversification to unrelated products
- Distinctive internal organization improvements

Figure 6.6   Business growth strategies

by the successor. Being able to benchmark with the firm's historic risk profile greatly eases the successor's task and leads to greater commitment to the growth strategy.

Intelligent growth of the enterprise helps ensure long-term survival of the family business and the new leader's sense of self-worth and value as a proven achiever.

Conclusion

This chapter explored how a development strategy can most effectively address the multiple and evolutionary challenges a family business encounters over time. The unconventional approach advocates an assertive role for the successor to break the deadlock between the generations. In order to be effective, however, the interests of all four constituencies – Family, Ownership, Management and the Individual – must be addressed. The issues can be meaningfully dealt with through a three-dimensional growth strategy. First, successors submit themselves to an individual growth process including in-depth learning and internal and external experience. Second, successors grow into their role as leaders through specialized guidance, developing their own agenda for the future and formally marking the passing of the baton of leadership. Third, the successor grows the business by intelligently linking tradition and innovation.

A growth-based initiative by the next generation recognizes succession as a phased process that begins with personal development and discipline. It is this humility, coupled with a transparent development process, which has the potential to obtain the support of family and others as the successor qualifies for the leadership position. Several successful family businesses have implemented this unconventional, but effective, successor development strategy to their firm's long-term benefit.

References

Hill, L. 2001. 'The brain and consciousness: sources of information for understanding adult learning,' in Merriam, S. (ed.), *The New Update on Adult Learning Theory*. San Francisco: Jossey-Bass; 73–81.

Kolb, D.A. 1984. *Experiential Learning: Experience on the Source of Learning and Development*. Englewood Cliffs: Prentice Hall.

7
Resolving Conflict in Family Businesses: Don't Be a Hostage to Family Harmony

George Kohlrieser

Working in a family business presents both unique opportunities and challenges. The fundamental desire to preserve harmony among family members can lead to complete conflict avoidance. There is a risk that both families and their businesses can be 'taken hostage,' resulting in a feeling of powerlessness or loss of control. Even in real-life hostage situations, the hostage has the power to influence and persuade the hostage-taker. Conflicts can be managed to raise and then resolve issues, thereby enhancing family harmony and protecting the long-term interests of both the family and the firm.

Families in business have special emotional attachments to each other and to their enterprise. Within the context of these emotional ties, people must communicate, lead, follow, be motivated, handle success or failure, and face daily challenges effectively. In addition, a family business must regularly deal with sensitive issues such as succession planning and family members' compensation. Family businesses can experience conflict more frequently than other types of organizations because of the complicated inner workings of any family that can result in sibling rivalry, children's desire to differentiate themselves from their parents, marital discord, identity conflict, and ownership dispersion among family members (Lubatkin *et al.*, 2001). The entire process is often emotionally charged and can quickly escalate into conflict and pain. Emotional issues can overrule economically rational behavior in a family business environment, giving rise to ill will that can fester for generations.

The ability of family members to face and resolve conflict is often constrained by the family's values and culture. Many families interpret conflict as a threat to harmony – a value that is perceived as essential to keeping the family together and one to be preserved at all costs. The fear of lost harmony and the associated pain are entirely normal. People are hard-wired to avoid pain and are likely to experience tension at the first sign of difficulty. Pain avoidance is an automatic, natural response that has helped humans through thousands of years to assess situations of potential danger. This response is the basis of the 'fight or flight' mechanism used to deal with threat or conflict.

When family members feel that conflict is imminent, they may continue to find reasons to avoid bringing problems into the open. For example, there may be a fear that confronting a family patriarch or a sibling will lead to increased tension. Family members may fear that open discussion of the issue may cause irreversible damage to the relationship. Fear of rejection, retaliation, embarrassment or humiliation or isolation may lead them to avoid conflict.

So how can family businesses learn to deal with the conflicts that will inevitably arise while maintaining a profitable, growing business? Some families instinctively avoid conflict altogether. But effective conflict management requires family members to draw boundaries between family and business spheres of activity and resolve problems from there. If not adequately addressed, family issues may spill over to the enterprise and endanger the life of the firm.

Effective conflict management involves important steps that may at first feel uncomfortable or inappropriate. For example, raising an issue, confronting a parent or giving unfavorable feedback may violate the family norms that have thus far maintained the dysfunctional family's interactions. Families that are proactive and address problems before they reach boiling point are generally more successful.

If the desire to protect family harmony leads to conflict avoidance, families may be 'taken hostage' to their fears and their desire to protect family harmony. This can happen any time their fears lead to feelings of entrapment, powerlessness, or ongoing resentment where nothing is done to solve the problem or where repeated attempts to solve the issue result in frustration and resentment. While some family situations may require professional counseling, conflict-management techniques used by hostage negotiators in dealing with real-life situations can provide powerful understanding and results.

The roots and nature of conflict

Conflict is a difference between two or more people characterized by tension, emotion, disagreement, and polarization and where bonding is either broken or lacking. At the root of all conflict is broken bonding. The bonding cycle is a powerful and fundamental concept that explains much about human behavior. Every relationship people have – whether minor, significant, temporary or long-lived, with animal or human (or even an object) – follows the pattern of the four-stage bonding cycle (see Figure 7.1).

- **Attachment**: When people first interact, and followed by a period of familiarization.
- **Bonding**: An exchange of energy taking place and mutual goals are established.
- **Separation**: A sense of loss and transition, a natural process since all bonds eventually lead to separation.
- **Grieving**: Enables all mammals to let go and make new attachments and ultimately experience renewal.

People have a basic need to seek proximity – that is, to be in the physical presence of another person, animal or object. Bonding is all about how people establish that proximity with each other, how they exchange energy and give a deeper sense of connectedness. It is crucial for people to learn to form and maintain connections in ways that allow relationships to exist even in the face of profound differences or serious conflict. This connection is then exhibited through a display of interest that allows people to bond. A person

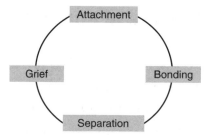

Figure 7.1   The four-stage bonding cycle

who is not bonded remains detached and emotionally disconnected and may eventually experience physical and psychological problems.

One common misconception is that people must like each other in order to bond. As hostage situations show, this is not necessary. What is important for both parties is a display of interest, an exchange of energy and a willingness to understand each other's needs. Successful leaders demonstrate the ability to bond and re-bond continually, and are also able to teach others. In order to be able to bond successfully, people must resolve any separation or grief issues from their past – otherwise they can find themselves repeating destructive behavior patterns over and over.

Unresolved separation or grief issues can lead to ongoing disruption that manifests itself through unhealthy behaviors such as addiction, depression, aggressive or violent actions and psychosomatic illnesses. In family businesses, and among family members, the appearance of such unhealthy behaviors can be seen as the individual's problem rather than as the effect of bonding issues, and therefore, effective assessment and resolution is not forthcoming.

For organizations and families to bond, there are five key steps: members must want to belong, they must be committed to common goals, they must communicate with mutual respect, they must be able to exhibit creative leadership and there must be maximum self-discipline.

Conflict of interests versus conflict of needs

Donohue and Kolt (1992) define conflict as 'a situation in which interdependent people express (manifest or latent) differences in satisfying their individual *needs and interests* and experience interference from each other in accomplishing their goals.' This definition frames several key thoughts regarding conflict.

While most conflict-management writers blend the concepts of interests and needs together, psychologists from Freud to Maslow point out an important distinction. Interests are viewed as more transitory and superficial, while needs are seen as more basic and enduring. Interests are tangible things that can be traded and compromised, such as land, money or jobs, while needs are intangible things that are not subject to negotiation, such as identity, security, respect or recognition.

Since needs are more intangible, they are often hidden beneath more visible conflicts over interests. But when human needs are in conflict too, simply resolving the conflict of interest will not make the friction go away. Sometimes, attempts to deal with the conflict of interest will actually make the situation worse, when, for example, people get angry at the thought of having to compromise. Similarly, the fundamental rule of 'separating the person from the problem' can also make matters worse as the identity of that person in relation to their role in the family may actually compound the problem.

Conflict-of-interest matters can often become emotional. It is not surprising that real or perceived conflicts of interest can lead to painful and emotional family battles. The issue of trust lies just below the surface. Pre-existing anger, resentment, perceived unfairness, pecking order issues, and communication breakdowns can be aggravated. The underlying problem is the assumption that such disputes are caused by the conflict of interests, when in reality it is a conflict of fundamental needs.

Usually conflicts cannot be adequately managed if needs remain repressed by the individual. Often ways can be found to meet these needs even without compromise. It is important to realize that in such situations, the people involved in the conflict are concerned by loss. Behind every need there is

Loss of attachment (who am I connected to?)	Need to feel connected/security
Loss of territory (where do I belong?)	Need to have a sense of belonging/grounding
Loss of structure (what is my role?)	Need to feel important and valued/involved
Loss of future (where am I going?)	Need to know where it is all leading to
Loss of meaning (what is the point?)	Need to attach meaning and purpose to the situation
Loss of control (I feel overwhelmed)	Need to feel in control of the situation/destiny

Figure 7.2 Types of loss and their roots

a fear of *loss*, real or perceived, as represented by the separation phase of the bonding cycle. Therefore, it is easier to resolve the issues if the parties involved in the conflict understand what is at stake.

Figure 7.2 outlines some of the examples of loss or need felt by people.

The complexity of family business impacts conflict

Conflict in family business comes with the territory (Ward, 1987). The fact that there are two very different value systems of human activity

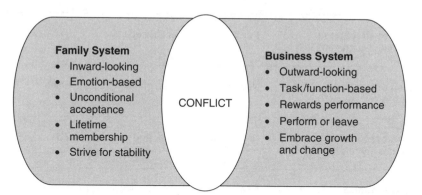

Figure 7.3 Contrasting spheres of family business activity from which conflict emerges

interacting – the family and the business – is the most obvious origin of conflict (see Figure 7.3).

The family unit is emotion-based. Its principle is loyalty and equality. Its purpose is to nurture and care for each other. Membership can be for life, regardless of performance. The problem begins where the two units overlap. The rules of the family generally contradict the rules of the business, and vice versa. The result is conflict. In addition, drivers of conflict in family business are individual personality clashes and variations among personal life cycles, family life cycles, and business life cycles.

Family and business value systems

Generally in business, the rules of interaction are based upon official standards of behavior and implicit or explicit contracts. In a family business, contracts between individuals are often unwritten and involve emotional ties, rather than legal ties. Even with non-family employees, paternalism is the norm rather than the exception. The threat of, or recourse to, a legal solution is avoided, or often assumed not to apply. This is both an advantage and a disadvantage for conflict management in family businesses. By avoiding legal proceedings, the transaction costs of managing conflict are kept low. The informal nature of decision-making in a family business means that conflicts that surface can be dealt with quickly according to the family's skill in handling conflict resolution.

The latter point is not always an advantage for people involved in a conflict. The disadvantage of such an unstructured approach to conflict management lies in the fact that when things go wrong, they can go drastically wrong, with major implications for both the family and the business. If conflict is repressed and avoided, family members may detach from each other and lose the bond that is crucial for keeping it all together. It puts the family and business at risk. Non-family employees will not feel included in the family decision-making process and their commitment to the company will likewise be eroded.

A strong and cohesive family culture provides a values-oriented framework that augments business performance. However, too close an entwining of family and business interests can give rise to authoritarian, informal or opaque decision-making that alienates or confuses some constituents. For example, conflict can arise from the dominant presence of the family – setting the rules and having ultimate power, the lack of formalized systems and structures to deal with conflict, and having no formal organizational structure or operative systems and the co-mingling of business and family roles (Harvey and Evans, 1994).

Arbitrary decisions based on maintaining family cohesion in the short term, at the expense of long-term business performance, follow from conflict avoidance. For example, promotion of an underqualified, but favored, family member by the matriarch of a family business may anger others (both family and non-family). However, the high value placed on family cohesion will often drive resistance to this decision underground, where it will fester under the surface, causing eventual untold damage to business performance. In such a case, many parties have been taken hostage by conflict avoidance.

Similarly, a retiring CEO (a father) may wish to appoint a highly effective non-family member as CEO. However, an offspring may consider it his birthright to become the next CEO. The father then decides in favor of the offspring in a bid to ensure connectedness with his child and grandchildren. He ultimately becomes a hostage.

There are innumerable examples in which the discipline and cohesion of a family has helped create superior firms. However, there are also many examples where conflict between family and business cultures has resulted in the break-up of a family business empire and the breakdown of family relationships.

Family and business life cycles

The impact of family and business life-cycle changes, such as the arrival of children, children joining the family business, and leadership succession, constitute significant sources of potential conflict. Recommended conflict-management techniques are far more effective if the parties involved understand their own sense of loss in the face of major events in the life of the family or company.

As members of family-owned businesses already share a blood bond, the dynamics of the bonding cycle related to business become even more complex.

Working in the family business makes it difficult to establish boundaries and come to grips with the reality of the cycle. For example, there may be an undercurrent of struggle between the younger generation and the senior generation over who is in charge and who knows best. This undercurrent is further fueled when the younger generation lobbies the parent for the legitimacy of its position. This dynamic, which is common in all families, now surfaces within the business context. The ambiguity of this situation is very difficult to work through and can create tremendous stress and frustrations.

When emotional pain resulting from any conflict is handled well, it is often accompanied by a willingness to re-enter a situation that might be painful and unpleasant, and confront it head on. People will have a feeling of satisfaction and pride if they see the pain as the necessary price to pay to accomplish some valued outcomes, such as better business performance and strengthened family commitment. As the saying goes, 'No pain, no gain.' But to reach this kind of outcome family members need to feel hope along the way – confidence and belief in the worth and achievability of the goal. When the inevitable emotions of frustration and anger surface, the family needs a leader who can guide them through a conflict-resolution process, intervening and dealing with the pain, as appropriate.

Time is viewed differently in the life of an individual and in the life of a business. This often means that the family life cycle is out of sync with that of the business (see Figure 7.4), representing another source of conflict. For example, as the founder's life as energetic president is coming to an end, he might still feel empowered by the position of being a family patriarch and feel that giving up this position will be a loss that he is not prepared to embrace. The reason has to do with the aging process. The inevitable loss of physical and mental capacities creates anxiety and tension along with an increasing and inescapable degree of dependence. Since most successful

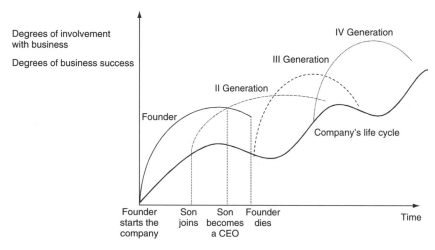

Figure 7.4 Family and business life cycles

business people have enjoyed an unusual degree of control over their lives, having to face the possibility that they may be losing control can be especially disconcerting. Paradoxically, one must feel secure, confident and independent in order to reach the point of no return when control goes out of one's hands into the hands of another.

Successors, at the same time, are keen to prove their worth. Not allowing them to step in at the appropriate moment to share power and responsibility can cause feelings of alienation. In companies with authoritarian control, compliance is expected and decisions are imposed from the top. Individuals lacking control over organizational processes feel anger and resentment. The more dependent these individuals are on the organization, the stronger their negative effect becomes when faced with undesirable outcomes (Johnson and Ford, 2000).

The feeling of lack of control is commonplace for family business successions. Controlling founders often establish norms, attitudes, and values

(Kets de Vries, 1993). They are rarely openly questioned (Beckhard and Dyer, 1983). As a result, a conflict might never resurface during their reign. For example, when dominant individuals are perceived to have high punitive capabilities within the organization and the family, the level of information exchanged can be extremely low (De Dreu *et al.*, 1998). Such groups must watch out for the lurking danger of unresolved issues.

When the time for generational transition arises but the founder has not planned for the continuity of the business, the next generation must face the reality that their choices may be limited. When the choice is that stark, the situation can easily come to the brink where the stress on the business and family relationships risks destroying them both. Starting the planning process as early as possible will help to minimize the conflict at a later stage.

Personality differences

Family businesses can promote cohesion, but they can also be hotbeds of conflict. Acting simultaneously as a family member and a business colleague can produce any number of problems (Jaffe, 1990; Rosenblatt *et al.*, 1985; Salganicoff, 1990). Consider the main players in family business conflicts as illustrated in Figure 7.5:

- Nuclear family members working in the business;
- Extended family members working in the business;
- Non-family employees;
- Family members (extended or otherwise) not working in the business.

Conflict can arise from interactions between or within any of these groups. The possible permutations are endless, with each group having to deal with

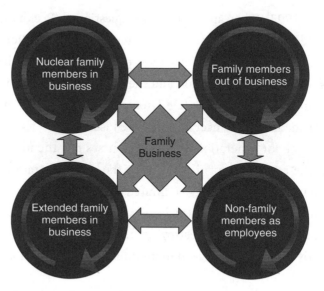

Figure 7.5   The main players in family business conflicts

its issues concerning inclusion or exclusion from decision-making processes. There is an incredible array of family business conflict sources.

Possible permutations of conflict in family business

When people enter a family business, they gain security and many other benefits. But there can also be significant psychological costs attached to this decision. A cost that no person should pay to join a family business is the sacrifice of his/her own identity. Self-esteem is critical to a life of independence and fulfillment, and it is derived from achievement and work. When individuals reach their mid-thirties, they typically develop a burning desire to move forward to test their own strength, to risk trusting their own judgment.

If the next generation in a family business is not allowed these developmental opportunities, anger and bitterness can result (Davidow and Narva, 2002a).

The gap in years, and the corresponding difference in life experiences between the generations can become a chasm dividing parents and children and the generations as each tries to communicate from its own frame of reference.

This dynamic applies not just to the inter-generational issue but to other family relationships as well. It may be difficult to work for one's father, but it may be impossible to work for one's brother or sister. The brother or sister who has never been in charge or who has never been autonomous is frequently a very unhappy person.

With such a large array of constituents, it is possible that what appears to be an isolated issue can escalate into a free-for-all conflict among factions that will result in broken bonding, negative feelings, suspicion and resentment. Given the seriousness of this issue, it becomes even more vital for leaders and managers in family businesses to develop a proactive approach to conflict resolution.

Dealing with conflict

In order to resolve conflict, it is necessary to create a bond with the other parties involved. It is not necessary to like someone to bond with them. Bonding is a powerful process that lays down the foundations for a successful outcome to any dispute or confrontation.

With the understanding of the roots and nature of conflict, there are six key steps to creating a bond that brings conflicts into the open and resolves them in a constructive and healthy manner.

(1) *Separate the person from the problem*: Issues cannot be resolved productively if there is disrespect between the parties. Blaming others solves nothing and abdicates control. This problem frequently develops when jealousy arises from the naming of a successor. Blame, even if it is deserved, only makes people more defensive. Even worse, blame may precipitate attacks in response and the conflict can worsen.

It is essential to understand the perspective of other relevant parties, so that their viewpoints can be taken into account. This means that family members must listen openly and actively to each other, reserving judgment and avoiding blame. To do this, it is necessary to focus on the problem not the person, maintaining respect for the individual and working together with common goals to find a resolution.

(2) *Master the mind's eye*: The mind's eye is physically located in the brain. It controls the way people view themselves and the world. If people have secure bases in the form of close bonds, they are then able to focus clearly on what they want to achieve. A secure base enables one to have a clear focus, shows interest and provides protection. Through this focus, people can monitor their behavior and determine the outcome of situations in a calm and controlled manner. If family members can visualize a successful outcome, they can avoid some of the tension and polarization often present in disagreements. The mindset with which people approach discord can radically alter the outcome for the positive. Many conflict theorists suggest that one should not think of conflict as either good or bad, but as an expression of differences. Disputes should be viewed as the way to make work what was failing and as a means to address unmet needs of those unhappy with the status quo. Yet in many family contexts, thinking about one's own needs and interests might seem selfish or inappropriate. But, focusing on one's needs is actually good for the family system as a whole. Taking stock

of the situation, assessing where the problem lies, and visualizing a positive outcome enables people to move in the right direction – from identifying the issue to actually raising it and dealing with it.

(3) *Manage dialogue with mutual respect*: Family members often begin a dialogue with the expectation that the other party should understand and become sympathetic to their position. This is especially relevant in cases of inter-generational conflict. One generation expects that the other should be willing to meet them at least half way. But the conversation frequently deteriorates because each generation expects the other to come not just half way. Neither is able to deliver because they cannot find the middle ground. When this happens, each side may feel disappointed, giving rise to anger and miscommunication.

If work colleagues have a concern or issue, it can hang over a team and often paralyze the group's productivity. It is far healthier and more effective to raise those concerns and work to a mutually beneficial conclusion. The words people use and stop using, can make a significant difference to business performance. In stressful situations, family members can speak to each other through a series of monologues. One person states his or her point of view, followed by the next person, followed by the next – a series of individual speeches joined only by a 'Yes, but.' Business conversations can become 'wars of words' or even worse, 'sieges of silence.' It is important that family members recognize and avoid dialogue blockers, so that they can engage in a true conversation.

(4) *Look at options and proposals*: When approaching family or organizational dissonance, it is important that the parties brainstorm together to generate a variety of possible resolutions. A number of options should be developed, shifting the immediate focus away from the entrenched positions with which the parties arrived. In a successful negotiation, both

parties decide, through conversation and dialogue, that they want the same thing. Being able to say, 'I want what you want' is a powerful way to get someone to see another's point of view.

(5) *The power of concession-making*: It is vital that all parties use respect and courtesy at all times, treating others as they would wish to be treated. One very powerful tool in conflict resolution is concession-making. If someone makes a concession, no matter how small, the other person should recognize the concession and reward it. Successful negotiations are often resolved through a series of small steps, and concession-making plays a key role in the process of continually moving the negotiation forward. People are able to see things more clearly and act more rationally when they feel they are respected. Conversely, it is often perceived disrespect that causes people to react with sudden and sometimes violent emotion. Unfortunately, many managers often view concessions as a sign of weakness. A negotiation is seen as an 'I win, you lose' scenario. However, reciprocity actually allows for a greater control over the conversation and enables family members to exhibit greater leadership. By being the first to make a concession, a family member can assist in keeping the conversation on a business-like footing. Making concessions sets the stage for a win–win outcome for all. Indeed, the art of concession-making is at the heart of all conflict resolution.

(6) *Maintain the relationship*: Having reached a general understanding of the resolution, a foundation for a new agreement can be formed. If family members have a formula for the dialogue that will maximize the potential for everyone, then agreements can become a reality. An important part of any agreement is the creation of a climate that encourages the repeated raising of issues in a constructive manner and framed in a dialogue of mutual respect.

Once a resolution is reached, or even attempted, it is valuable to communicate it to others in the family and, as relevant, with other managers. The goal is to build a culture of conflict acceptance and management. With each success comes an increased capacity to deal with difference positively. Ideally, addressing conflict will become a proud challenge and a source of competitive advantage for the family business.

When family members approach a divergence of views with mutual respect, they may then be emboldened to devote energy to resolving new issues. Family members will have a new and profound sense of freedom because they have raised previously unspoken concerns. They can then deal with issues from the past, move on from the separation and grieving stages of the bonding cycle, and re-bond in a way that provides a new hope and empowerment for the future.

Organizational cultures in general, and family business cultures in particular, are largely determined by precedent. Culture has been described simply as 'the way things are done around here' and is made up of collective memories of past challenges, decisions and events. By adding a new dynamic of embracing conflict and widely circulating news of its successful resolution, a corporate culture can be transformed or preserved.

There are both formal and informal ways to communicate this news. Word of mouth is one way. Newsletters and formal presentations can also do the job. Whichever way is selected, ultimately, much depends on the family culture and the effect that it has on the way individuals perceive their role in the business and decision-making processes. Publicizing the precedent is important in establishing a more cohesive family culture and creating a culture that is more trusting and cooperative, fundamental prerequisites for real family harmony.

Reciprocal obligations

Compared with non-family enterprises, members of family firms more often feel an obligation to be sensitive to the needs of others. Reciprocal obligations are a uniquely defining feature of family relationships (Davidow and Narva, 2002b). But, ironically, it is this sense of obligation that can block meaningful dialogue and make people feel hostage to their position within the family. Each member has to sort out his or her own obligation to the business, and the family. It is normal for family business members to feel a sense of obligation to themselves, the business, and their family – choosing between them can be difficult. A resulting sense of helplessness can lead family members to avoid dialogue altogether. The reality is that such discussions are problematic because family members have problems facing the real issues. For the older generation, it involves dealing with aging, ceding power and control, and preparing for death and loss. For the successors, it means growing up to accept responsibility.

'Put the fish on the table'

One of the most effective methods to resolve conflict involves learning to put the fish on the table. Think of the seaside market where, early in the morning, fishermen bring their harvest of fresh fish to the shore. The air is crisp and clear but soon it is impregnated with a healthy fishy smell coming from the stalls of the merchants picking up their daily supplies. Before the fish gets to the customer it has to be cleaned. If the fishermen do not under-take this unpleasant task, no one will get the benefit of a great dinner at the end of the day.

The motivation to 'clean the fish' of family conflict is critical. There must be something truly vital at stake for family members to give the process of 'putting the fish on the table' their undivided attention. There must be a positive reward of a 'great dinner' in order for the contentious and perhaps painful process of facing and resolving conflict to be worthwhile. The ultimate reward is the continuity of the family enterprise, the consequences are too dire to contemplate. Of course, there are other rewards and consequences with less severe implications. But the survival of the business is critical on so many fronts and is one that all family members can understand.

Family must make it a rule to 'put the fish on the table' and detail all aspects of the issues they face. This way they can treat the conflict as an issue of global concern to the group and work together to find a solution. As idealistic as it sounds, this method actually works almost every time. When individuals are involved in tense situations with others, they are not always at their rational best. Stress causes people to shift to a more emotional frame of mind and simply recognizing this may help generate positive outcomes. It helps to learn and firmly follow the 'rules' of 'putting the fish on the table.'

- Recognize and admit to a growing problem while it is still minor and be willing to discuss it. Do not harbor complaints – either raise issues in a non-accusatory manner when they occur or drop them altogether.
- Choose topics for discussion thoughtfully and carefully. Take time to clarify feelings before reacting. On emotionally charged issues, rehearse, if possible, before making a statement.
- When stating a point of view, be mindful of your tone of voice and that of the person with whom you are communicating.

- Focus on the issue, not on personalities or on the past.
- Put objections in question form as often as possible (What would you think if...? Have you considered the possibility...? Would it work if...?). Always offer an alternative as a different way of thinking about the problem, if an objection is raised.
- Minimize the negative and maximize the positive, by acknowledging and reinforcing cooperation and concessions.
- Help the other person save face whenever possible by offering choices and compromising when it does not violate one's own rights.
- Use the problem to discover the other person's thinking rather than as an occasion to win.
- Avoid blocks to dialogue – i.e., passivity, sarcasm, discounting, etc., particularly the use of the phrase 'Yes, but.'

There are family businesses that prefer not to put their emotions on display. However, family members should be aware that the person who tries to 'put the fish on the table' may feel he or she stands to lose the most if a decision is not made or inaction results. When conflicts occur and disputes surface, deal with them quickly and directly by 'putting the fish on the table.' Then discuss the matter at a family meeting so the entire group will understand the problem and support the ultimate solution.

The following are examples of difficult situations:

- The person acknowledging the problem might be the founder who is afraid of alienating the eldest son when the youngest is made president. The founder can no longer delay making the decision as an announcement is expected at the upcoming board meeting.
- The founder's daughter threatens to leave the company if her merits are not acknowledged in the form of serious promotion or extension of her

responsibilities. It might be that the daughter can no longer wait for promises to be fulfilled. She has been offered an attractive position at another corporation and must give her answer within three days. If she stays, her bargaining position with the father might weaken and the chances of resolving their emotional issues will disappear. On the other hand, if she leaves the family business it might shatter any hopes of resolution.

- A spouse feels that being forced into a position where he or she has to take sides and advocate in favor of one family member against another is not fair.

If these issues are not given proper attention, families will never arrive at the point of resolving conflict until it is (almost) too late.

The most effective way to defuse serious issues is for each member of the family to agree upon and participate in a sustained family dialogue. It may be necessary to use experts to facilitate the dialogue in the beginning, or at points along the way. During this dialogue, the actual process of communication is extremely important.

At the same time, real family business issues can be discussed. For example, the family should examine and deal with the issues of future leadership and compensation. By putting issues 'on the table,' with constructive dialogue, families can go a long way toward easing tensions in the future.

In the mid-1990s, Sam, just a few years into his tenure as CEO, started to spend much more time in the marketing department than he had in the past. His presence had the effect of distorting reporting relationships within the department and severely undercutting the authority of his own brother, David, who was the marketing boss.

Sam's involvement resulted in millions of dollars poured into products that many in the marketing department felt should have died an earlier death.

In the meantime, the other two brothers – Scott and David – who had had their differences in the past, were united in believing that Sam should no longer be in charge of the company, and began gathering evidence to make their case to the company's directors without confronting Sam directly.

Before they had their chance, however, Sam anticipated the attack and brought the matter to a head at a fateful September board meeting. Sam, backed by his father, argued that the board should remove David and his supporters for undermining his authority. David and Scott, both directors, were asked to leave the room while the board (four of nine members were not family-related) decided their fate. The votes were cast in favor of the CEO, and David was asked to resign. Scott was then given the option to stay, so long as he signed a document promising to abandon all efforts to remove Sam. Instead, he too chose to resign. The company experienced major turmoil for many years and Sam no longer had any communication with his brothers.

In this case, it would be appropriate for the father to try and see the situation from his son's perspective. He does not have to agree with his perception of the situation. But it is important to understand what he thinks and feels.

Secondly, the father should not deduce the son's intentions from his own fears. This sort of suspicious attitude makes it difficult to accurately assess the son's real intentions.

The father should take the initiative to discuss the matter with his son. Explicit discussion of each side's perceptions can help both sides to better understand each other. Also, such discussion may reveal a common viewpoint. Acknowledging shared perceptions can strengthen relationships and facilitate productive negotiations (Ury, 1993).

There are lots of theories and mechanisms that enable family businesses to plan better to avoid potentially fatal outcomes not only for the business but also for the family. But every small conflict that can be resolved together today will eventually pave the way for dealing more effectively with the differences that are an inevitable part of tomorrow.

When engaged in conflict, it is difficult for anyone to effectively 'put the fish on the table' and subsequently reconcile the conflict. The natural biases and anger on both sides work to the detriment of the conflict-management process. This is where third-party involvement can be helpful in assisting families to work together toward a resolution. The outside party should enter the negotiation, making clear their position of neutrality and their desire to work through the conflict cycle toward a successful resolution. The individual should act as a facilitator in the conflict-management process and remain neutral throughout to ensure that all parties are brought closer together rather than farther apart. Neutrality gives each side hope for a fair outcome.

This is not to say that families should seek to remove the emotional power of familial relationships from their businesses. Rather, to manage the process successfully, owners, managers and advisors to the business must recognize the power of those relationships. Regardless of size, a family business will at some point become a stage on which the emotional dramas of the owning family are played out. This reality must be understood for conflicts to be managed in a way that allows the family business to prosper.

Ury (1993) outlines five clear steps of breakthrough in negotiations that will help to ensure that issues do not get driven back underground and that the outcome of any dialogue is satisfactory:

- Do not react to provocation. Step away from the scene, calm down, and carefully plan your response. Do not respond automatically, because most knee-jerk responses are negative and may further escalate the situation.
- Step around obstacles, do not walk right into them. Use active listening to defuse negative feelings, and use 'I-messages' to express your feelings. Agree whenever you can, but stand up for your principles as well.
- Ask people 'Why?,' 'Why not?' or 'How is that fair?' to try to move the people involved away from positional bargaining toward principled negotiation.
- Make it easy for your opponent to agree by making the offer as attractive as possible.
- 'Bring them to their senses, not their knees.'

In the 'heat of the moment,' this commonsense advice can be more difficult to apply than it sounds. However, by following and practicing the steps outlined in this chapter, families can take greater control of themselves and the situation, ensuring that they resist being taken hostage by any situation.

Conclusion

Since preserving family harmony figures as a key goal in family businesses, the ability to successfully manage conflict becomes an invaluable skill. Unresolved conflict threatens both the business and the family – a most treasured and profound relationship.

The opportunities for conflict abound in enterprising families. Families in business face the monumental challenge of balancing family and business interests.

Further complications inherent in such complex scenarios include personal, family and business hurdles and are rarely synchronized. If they were it would be more by coincidence as each life cycle has its own independent time horizon.

Dissonance is further exacerbated by the intensity of personal relationships and the implications for other family members – spouses, grandchildren and even generations to come. With conflict so endemic and the stakes so high, families need to have a thorough grasp of its roots and nature and the skills to manage it. It is also extremely important to raise family members' awareness of how being a family adds special challenges and counterintuitive thinking to managing conflict.

Unfortunately, individuals instinctively avoid conflict, and families seem to be even more fearful of its potentially disruptive consequences. With family harmony so essential, avoidance appears desirable, and compromise, appropriate.

It is clear that successful family businesses are able to effectively address conflict. They have learned the importance of managing discord and know how to apply the essential skills, such as the ability to 'put the fish on the table,' in a timely and constructive way.

Many conflict-management techniques jump too quickly to the process of negotiating personal interests – seeking win–win outcomes. However, there is a key step that should come first. Family members need to understand that it is not just different interests that are at the core of conflict, but also needs and fears of personal loss. By examining the underpinnings of loss in this chapter, people may identify the real fears at work in their interactions.

The next step may feel even more counterintuitive to families. Start by offering one's own needs and fears of loss first. Most would believe that revealing personal fears is inappropriate in a family or in a negotiation of interests. On the contrary, it takes special courage and skill to open discussions by sharing needs and fears. Taking that perceived risk actually brings more hope and greater possibilities of resolution. Displaying vulnerability makes it easier for everyone to more quickly 'put the fish on the table.'

Certainly there will be times when conflict is so painful and personal that professional intervention is required. In this case, it is critical to reach out to get the process started.

By understanding the roots and nature of conflict, and by then creating a climate in which family members and employees feel secure in raising personal concerns and fears, family businesses can successfully resolve conflict and ensure the preservation of family harmony and the long-term viability of both the family and the business.

References

Beckhard, R. and Dyer, W.G., Jr. 1983. 'SMR Forum: managing change in the family firm – issues and strategies.' *Sloan Management Review*, 24: 59–65.

Davidow, T.D. and Narva, R.L. 2002a. Making peace between the generations in family businesses. <http://www.genusresources.com/site/content/publications/articles/davidow_narva_peace.asp>

Davidow, T.D. and Narva R.L. 2002b. The key issues that can help family businesses gain control of sibling rivalries. <http://www.genusresources.com/site/content/publications/articles/davidow_narva_sibling.asp>

De Dreu, C.K.W., Giebels, E. and Van de Vliert, E. 1998. 'Social motives and trust in integrative negotiation: the disruptive effects of punitive capability.' *Journal of Applied Psychology*, 83(3): 408–422.

Donahue, W.A. and Kolt, R. 1992. *Managing Interpersonal Conflict*. London: Sage Publications.

Harvey, M. and Evans, R.E. 1994. 'Family business and multiple levels of conflict.' *Family Business Review*, Vol. 7, Iss. 4: 331–348.

Jaffe, D.T. 1990. *Working with the Ones You Love: Conflict Resolution & Problem Solving Strategies for a Successful Family Business*. Berkeley: Conari Press.

Johnson, C. and Ford, R. 2000. 'Emotional reactions to conflict: do dependence and legitimacy matter?' *Social Forces*, 79(1): 107–138.

Kets de Vries, M.F.R. 1993. 'The dynamics of family controlled firms: the good and the bad news.' *Organizational Dynamics*, 21(3): 59–71.

Lubatkin, M.H., Schulze, W.S., Dino, R.N. and Buchholtz, A.K. 2001. 'Agency relationships in family firms: theory and evidence.' *Organization Science*, Vol. 12, Iss. 2: 99.

Rosenblatt, P.C., de Mik, L., Anderson, R.M. and Johnson, P.A. 1985. *The Family in Business*. San Francisco: Jossey-Bass.

Salganicoff, M. 1990. 'Women in family business: challenges and opportunities.' *Family Business Review*, Vol. 3, Iss. 2: 125–138.

Ury, W. 1993. *Getting Past No: Negotiating Your Way from Confrontation to Cooperation*. New York: Bantam.

Ward, J.L. 1987. *Keeping the Family Business Healthy: How to Plan for Continuing Growth*. San Francisco: Jossey-Bass.

8
Effective Family Communications: It's Not What's Said That's Important, But What's Heard

Jean L. Kahwajy

When a tree falls in the forest, and no one hears it, does it actually fall? The answer to this riddle depends on the motivation of the questioner. Meaning lies in people's intentions, not their words. Language is merely one conduit with which humans create relationships, connections and, ultimately, if very lucky, shared understanding.

Wanting to understand and be understood is the first step in dialogue and is an affirmative choice. As a choice, it is in each individual's complete control. Each can open himself to understanding and can also invite the acquaintance of others. This epiphany – moving from reluctance to extend one's self to a sincere desire to understand – is independent of past experiences and even initial inclinations. Which party extends the invitation, what precipitates the need for a conversation and how the overture is made, are dynamics that are often counterintuitive and misunderstood. In fact, individuals often operate in opposition to these key dynamics by unknowingly and unintentionally building barriers to understanding when, instead, they seek to build bridges. Further, when a breakdown in communication happens, those attempting to communicate look to the wrong side of the interaction for the solution – the other person. In this way, preconceptions become a self-fulfilling prophecy (Merton, 1948). In abdicating their role in ameliorating the situation, they leave to chance the resolution. And, if they think they know the other person well, as among family members, there is an even higher risk of approaching interactions with rigid expectations. Such a self-imposed barrier can blind individuals to their responsibility in the dialogue and prevents them from playing a necessary and critical role. Moreover, people are frequently oblivious to the impact of their words and actions, thus making this an even more difficult obstacle to overcome.

Conflict, when someone's opinion or belief is in opposition to our own, is often viewed as an obstacle to communication. However, conflict is a necessary prerequisite to a conversation. People ought not to wish for the absence of conflict, but rather to realize that conflict is the mechanism that invites discussion; it provides a basis for conversation by offering the potential for updated understanding. If there is no basis for dialogue, people need not engage another. What kind of conflict, then, gains a foundation for communicating? And why is conflict a necessary precondition to effective communication? Communication boils down to the understanding of difference – in knowledge, in intimacy. Conversation truly begins when two people hold their own views but maintain an openness to hearing new ideas and potentially having these new ideas update their own understanding.

Dialogue is often viewed as an activity requiring mutual consent. But if we think about what precedes it, one person usually has a purpose for interacting with another and can initiate the willing participation of both parties. The first task is to get the other interested, in spite of insidious perceptions and biases that can limit interaction. People possess their own unique set of experiences that color the way they perceive and interpret the world. But healthy, productive communication merely requires the willing participation of both parties who must want and struggle to achieve mutual understanding.

It only takes one

So how many people does it take to initiate a great conversation? One person with a purpose. Necessity is always present in interactions and is, in fact, the reason for communication. However, what often goes wrong is that both parties bring with them a host of misperceptions. Past experiences, expectations and biases that generally escape notice limit the potential of the encounter. When people are stereotyped, their potential contributions and viewpoints are unintentionally excluded. This may be especially prevalent in families since they have spent their lives together, and labeling (like 'the smart one,' 'the favorite') is likely to have occurred long before. Creating excuses for behavior or narrowly focusing on performance hamstrings communication and blocks participation. Getting to the core of how this negative spiral is perpetuated, ironically by those who can most benefit, is essential. The problem is not conflict, but rather that differing perceptions of the world frustrate our ability to effectively respond to it.

Individuals tend to focus on the content – the 'what' of an interaction rather than on the 'how.' In attempting to convince someone of the veracity of one's argument, a 'push' approach based on justification of the position is common. When someone's input or perspective is sought, a 'pull' approach is more natural and elicits listening and participation. The first tactic is called proving and the latter, learning. The defensive posture inherent in the 'push' approach may be more common in family groups due to the overwhelming influence of the hierarchical relationships typical in families. Why are human beings programmed to naturally fall into the proving mode? Does the learning approach lead to better outcomes? If so, why is it so difficult?

Beliefs, biases and the self-fulfilling prophecy

Attempting to understand another is complicated – people tend to find what they expect. Information processing is selective in that (Nisbett and Ross, 1980):

- We see what we are prepared to see (biased assimilation);
- We interpret what we want to interpret (belief perseverance).

Beliefs not only affect how events are seen and interpreted but can also create reality itself. What we expect to see happens, as illustrated in Figure 8.1 (Jones, 1986).

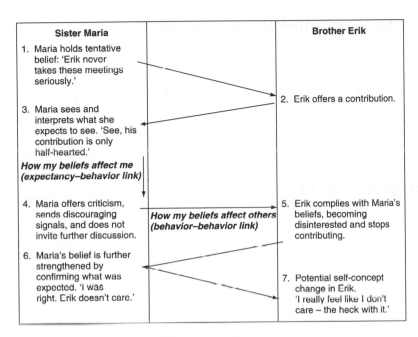

Figure 8.1 How expectations affect interactions

Destroying or leaving value on the table

In interactions and especially in negotiations, value can be unintentionally destroyed or left on the table by:

- Specific expectations that predetermine a particular role, response or outcome;
- Independent thinking;
- Assumptions made about the motivations of others;
- The presumption that people should anticipate each other's desires.

Hence, an open attitude and modifiable intention fail to be cultivated.

The proving and learning roads

Pursuing the 'proving road' or the 'learning road' is a choice that can either facilitate or block learning. Blaming external forces is a tell-tale sign.

The proving road

- Advice giving
- Selling
- Judging and evaluating
- Thinking right/wrong, good/bad

  - Was I right?
  - Did I win?
  - Was I thinking on my own?
  - Did I do all the work?

There are indications that the proving road is being pursued:

- Being defensive

  - Using arguments, justifications, excuses.

- Sympathizing

  - 'You'll feel different tomorrow.'
  - 'Things will get better.' 'It is not that bad.'

- Advising

    - 'What I think you should do is.'
    - 'It will be best for you.'
    - 'Calm down.'

- Stating your judgment as fact

    - 'You have misunderstood me.' 'You are wrong.'
    - 'That is a really stupid thing to say.'

It is also quite easy to unintentionally go down the proving road:

- Being nice (rather than kind)

    - Saying what we think others want us to say.
    - Not telling the truth.

- Monologuing (rather than dialoguing)

    - One-way communication.
    - 'Leading the witness.'
    - This often occurs when we have a particular response or outcome
      in mind.

What problems are associated with the proving road?

- Other people are excluded along with their unanticipated contributions.
  Thus, others are not encouraged to contribute or engage.
- Individuals are not open to receiving when they unknowingly
  control the situation, want predetermined outcomes or discourage
  creativity.

The learning road

To be on this road entails:

- Active listening
- Wanting to grow
- Being open to finding out more
- Being engaged and engaging
- Being involved and committed
- Inviting participation
- Being affected by the situation
- Wanting to change me, not others or the situation

To get on the learning road:

- Share information with an openness toward personal learning;
- Explain the personal impact ('I experience it/you this way,' 'I have a problem with this');
- Share information, not judgment ('I am confused when....' rather than 'You confuse me');
- Speak from a personal perspective and share information and circumstances.

The language of learning

Figure 8.2 gives some examples of how to phrase questions to achieve positive results. But how can this help in a difficult situation? Rather than wishing that the situation were different, figure out how to manage through it with the best response.

How we act determines the response		
'I think that . . .' 'I want to tell you . . .' 'I have difficulty understanding you . . .' 'I am interested to hear how you see it.'	rather than	'Everyone thinks that . . .' 'I was told to tell you . . .' 'No one can understand you . . .' Justify what you are thinking.
When asking questions, interaction is invited by being open-ended		
'What questions do you have?' 'How can I help you?'	rather than	'Do you have any questions?' 'Can I help you?'
Clearly and authentically ask for what is wanted		
'What do you think?' 'Will you help me?'		
State your situation with an openness to participation		
'I don't know. Can we think on this together?' 'I am calling to confirm (not remind).' Make a request, not a demand.		

Figure 8.2 Communicating more effectively

- *What do I want?* The willing support and cooperation of others, their participation and goodwill.
- *Who is in a position to go first?* The person who has something to give or get.
- *How?* By recognizing that there are two sides to every interaction.

  1. Frame myself back into the situation.

     - *How?* By deciding to be open, to see beyond my current biases and beliefs, by my willingness to be wrong.

2. Focus on my side of the interaction and then inviting the other to want to participate.

   – *How*? By deciding to be modifiable, to be ready to update my own beliefs, by a readiness to change.

Because families know each other so well, more clues to an individual's real intentions are garnered than simply from words. Relatives are attuned to look for body language and other non-verbal forms of communication that confirm what is expected and can justify beliefs. This happens when people are unknowingly on the proving road. Positive change is possible only when one participant adopts a learning approach.

It is all but impossible to imagine a person approaching a social situation without some expectations. The problem arises when expectations are incorrect, limited or incomplete, which is usually the case. Beliefs can blind and secretly hold people hostage to past situations and experiences.

Being open to seeing beyond one's expectations – actively seeking new data to update beliefs – is an important first step. Consciously seeking to update expectations welcomes the unanticipated contributions of others. Specifically, being open indicates a willingness to participate and being modifiable invites others to participate with us, resulting in a genuine atmosphere of authentic communication.

The difference in approach can be subtle, but it can lead to vastly different outcomes (see Table 8.1).

Results from a series of studies show statistically significant improvements in interaction outcomes as well as in perceptions of the two interacting parties when one person approaches the situation with an attitude of openness and with the intention of being modifiable (Kahwajy, 2000).

Table 8.1 Non-receiving approach versus receiving approach

Non-receiving approach	Receiving approach
Do you have any questions?	What questions do you have?
I do not understand.	Will you help me understand?
I'm sorry I'm late.	Thank you for waiting.
As you recall, . . .	Do you recall . . . ?
You confuse me.	I am confused.
The dessert was good.	I enjoyed the dessert very much.

These experiments have confirmed that changing the attitude and intentions of someone with less authority could create changes in someone of more authority. These studies focus on a surprising actor, the target of the low expectations who is most aware of the discrepant beliefs, and on a surprising behavior, one of learning rather than of proving as a mechanism to update erroneous expectations and alter situational outcomes.

While change to more positive communication styles is a worthy objective, for families it may represent an elusive goal but an ever important one. Changing ingrained patterns of relating can be difficult. Maintaining more evolved relationships, even more so. Families, as a bulwark of stability and tradition in society, resist change.

Conclusion

The approach outlined here is not about getting rid of beliefs or expectations. Rather, it is about focusing on being willing to see beyond current beliefs and negotiating another's attention, participation and goodwill. It is also about inviting another to want to see beyond their initial beliefs. By adopting this simple but powerful approach, value can be created and better relationships may be fostered.

The psychological underpinnings of behaviors that can successfully engage another and capture loyalty, point to an interesting paradox. Even though there are two sides to every interaction, family relationships routinely condition us to see only one side clearly – to focus on the 'giver' and to ignore the role of the 'receiver.' This oversight can be tragic, especially as 'receiving' plays a key, but unheralded, role in all interactions. Individual contributions are not offered until they are specifically invited by a willing 'receiver' and go unnoticed until the 'receipt' is acknowledged. In this way, the 'receiver' is capable of encouraging contributions from the 'giver.'

Three obstacles commonly prevent all people – especially family relations – from being effective 'receivers.' First, selective information processing hampers attempts to correctly diagnose and fix problems. People see only what they expect and unknowingly dismiss input that does not confirm their expectations. Second, not only do beliefs affect what individuals see and how they interpret it, beliefs also automatically affect how they behave. A family member who offers criticism to another's behavior will undoubtedly find evidence of that behavior. This 'self-fulfilling prophecy' (Merton, 1948) can actually create reality. Third, human beings are typically unaware of these obstacles to communication.

Awareness of the dynamics at work in communication can increase the chances of more favorable outcomes for all. Not only may more valuable ideas and results emerge, but also more mutual goodwill and understanding.

References

Jones, E.E. 1986. 'Interpreting interpersonal behavior: the effects of expectancies.' *Science*, Vol. 234: 41–46.

Kahwajy, J.L. 2000. 'Toward a theory of social receiving: effects of target openness and modifiability on expectancy confirmation processes.' Dissertation, Stanford University, Stanford, CA.

Merton, R.K. 1948. 'The self-fulfilling prophecy.' *Antioch Review*, Vol. 8: 193–210.

Nisbett, R.E. and Ross, L. 1980. *Human Inference: Strategies and Shortcomings of Social Judgment*. Englewood Cliffs, NJ: Prentice-Hall.

9
The Family Constitution: It's the Process That Counts, Not the Content

John L. Ward

Drafting a family constitution is perhaps the most popular prescription given to business-owning families today. Family-business publications are aggressively promoting the idea, many consultants offer templates for ready-made constitutions, and an increasing number of professional service firms are touting their skill in helping families choose the values and policies that belong in successful constitutions.

IMD surveys show approximately 15% of all later-generation business families claim to have a family constitution. And more than half the families participating in IMD's Leading the Family Business program are engaged in writing at least part of a family constitution. Expectations are high: families are banking on their constitutions to prevent feuds among current family owners and to engender a passion for the business among future descendents. Done well, a family constitution can indeed build the requisite trust, unity, and enthusiasm to keep the business in the family's hands for generations to come.

Unfortunately, like most new management fashions, the advertised benefits of a family constitution are not that easy to achieve. Many families go through the trouble of writing a constitution, only to place it on a shelf untouched. When some ignore the policies the family has hammered out – not surprisingly – the rest become cynical about the family's capacity to grow and perform, and faith in the family's leaders wanes as well as optimism and energy for the business. Sometimes, even the process of writing the document creates more problems than it solves, especially when the family's business leaders take charge of drafting policies with dispatch, much to the resentment and suspicion of passive family owners.

Why do so many families founder when writing their constitutions? The primary reason is that they are too focused on the content of the document rather than on the process of developing it. An IMD research study suggests that the actual policies a family includes in its constitution are not nearly as important as how the rules fit the family and its business: the self-awareness of the family, how the family perceives the rules and renews them, the procedure for adopting the constitution, and the creative capacity of the family to reconcile the opposing needs and interests of family members and the business.

The typical approach

The family business leader is usually the one rallying the family to create a constitution. Naturally he takes great pride and responsibility for the success of the company – and does not necessarily view other family owners as an asset to the business. No one need remind him that family demands and conflicts can compromise the business's viability and threaten its survival. What is needed to ensure the company's continuity, he reasons, are clear rules that regulate family behavior – or at least insulate the business from the personal needs of family members. No longer will certain individuals see the company as honoring bloodlines over competence when they come up against the stiff requirements for employment and promotion the business leader envisions he will write in the constitution.

To this end, the business leader asks a trusted advisor, likely the company's lawyer, to draft policies that address such issues as family employment, ownership transfer and share redemption, dividends, and voting agreements. By dint of his persuasive skills or position of power, the business leader gets family members to view the document as a fait accompli and they sign off without comment. The process takes no time at all – three months compared to the two or three years it would have taken to involve all family members in drafting a constitution.

A family business agreement created by decree rather than consensus, however, is headed for trouble. Since it is impossible to anticipate every issue that will require a policy, a family constitution is forever a work in progress. And when family members are denied the experience of drafting the constitution together, they will not have the framework or problem-solving skills to tackle new challenges as they arise. Nor can the business leader accurately project the long-term consequences of the policies he establishes today. An entrepreneur with 100% of the shares may feel he should make decisions about ownership succession for family members. By the third generation, however, the issues are very different.

Another danger of a business leader assuming responsibility for the family's constitution is that the rest of the family may become complacent about the future of the business, believing that the mere presence of a constitution is an insurance policy for continued success.

Each of the assumptions the business leader in our example has made about family constitution 'best practices' is flawed: that rules prevent problems and should be implemented promptly; that policy-making is a management task; and that a quasi-contractual document with no revision provisions will protect the family and the business from future conflicts or discord. The strongest message this constitution conveys is that the drafters were more concerned with protecting the business than nurturing the family. The family, then, cannot help but get defensive and feel alienated from the business – attitudes that undoubtedly *will* encourage family members to view the company as a means for personal gain rather than a source of pride. This family constitution has effectively backfired.

The importance of family constitutions

The wisest advice a business family will get is to set policies governing the interface between the family and its business *before* problems occur. A family constitution is the ideal vehicle for family members to anticipate potentially contentious issues and decide as a group how to handle them. With concrete policies contained in a constitution, the family has the assurance that problems will be resolved quickly and that decisions will be consistently applied to each member. Written policies also help manage family expectations on certain topics – marriage contracts, for example – so that controversy over the issue never even emerges. (See Figure 9.1 for a list of family business policies.)

Governance	• Criteria for board members • Make-up of board • Frequency of family meetings • Membership criteria for family council or family association • Funding of family meetings • Communications and relationships between board and family and management • Strategic goals (i.e., growth, debt, etc.) for business • Selection of professional advisors • Successor selection process
Employment	• Qualifications • Conditions (i.e., leaves, part-time, etc.) • Reporting relationships • Compensation and benefits and perks and expenses • Performance review • Titles • Severance • Retirement
Ownership and Financial Planning	• Conditions for ownership and voting rights • Dispute resolution process • Dividends • Redemption process • Business valuation methodology • Estate plan communications and coordination and agreements • Buy–sell agreement • Insurance plans • Marriage contract arrangements • Rights and responsibilities of non-employed owners • Rules for joint travel • Addressing family member financial distress
Interpersonal Relationships	• Conflict resolution • Decision-making process • Conduct with each other and in public • Conflict of interest and non-compete
Company Conduct	• Information disclosure and public visibility • Charitable giving • Civic role support for owners and managers

Figure 9.1   Family business policies

Family constitutions also offer the family an exciting and compelling vision for the future and an invaluable source of family unity and pride. When future generations inevitably grumble, 'Why are we working so hard to keep this business?' they can find the answer – and renewed energy and motivation – in the family's stated principles of belonging to something larger than one's self and the pursuit of a meaningful purpose. A family constitution not only shapes each generation's expectations for their roles in the family business and as owners, it also inspires confidence among non-family managers and business partners that the owners are standing shoulder to shoulder with a game plan for the future.

Family and personal growth are other byproducts of forging a family constitution. Family members engaged in the important project of collectively deciding how the business entrusted to them will affect their lives, fortunes, and the family legacy cannot help but gain a deeper understanding of the needs and perspectives of individual family members as well as greater self-knowledge. They also receive an education in the operations of the family firm, family history and behavior patterns, and the evolution of the business. And the skills they must develop or hone to write a constitution – problem-solving, decision-making, listening, and communicating – will serve them well in all aspects of life.

But a constitution is only as valuable as the process it takes to create it. Constitutions drafted by the entire family with multiple members assuming leadership roles will deliver innumerable benefits – and demand considerable work. Convening family members for half a dozen or so meetings takes a great deal of time, which can frustrate the action-oriented, busy business leader. The deliberateness of the drafting also risks not having answers before issues arise. But a family that does not shortchange the process will build a more durable family constitution, greater family harmony, and the confidence that the family has the skills and fortitude to face future challenges, whatever they may be. Both the business and the family stand a good chance of not only enduring but thriving.

Although counterintuitive at first, the following strategies will enable families to create family constitutions that work and will stand the test of time.

Focus on family first

It all starts with the critical perspective that a family constitution's primary purpose is to support the family and help assure its continuity – not to protect the business and its future. Therefore, the term 'family constitution' is preferred over the more common 'Family Business Protocol.' When family welfare comes first, paradoxically, the family will eagerly support the welfare of the business.

Family constitutions that are designed to protect the business from family problems eventually provoke family problems that distract from the business. If the family feels secure that its interests are addressed, however, then it can readily accept sacrifice for the benefit of the business.

Start with family leadership

It is no surprise that the family's business leaders usually want to grab hold of the family constitution to ensure that the 'project' is managed efficiently. After all, they are natural leaders who care for the business and have experience channeling ambiguity and uncertainties into resolution and clear answers.

Unfortunately, their strong and skilled leadership silences the perspectives and participation of other family members. Business leaders also have limited tolerance for processes that focus on feelings and relationships or that are intended to develop leadership skills in family members without management experience. And business leaders usually fail to take into account how changing family dynamics and circumstances – new in-laws, death, personal problems – will stretch out the time needed to complete a family constitution.

For the constitution to be accepted and respected as the governing document for the entire family, the family must establish its own leadership *before* the process of writing the constitution can commence.

So where does the family find its leaders? If a family member has the instinct for leadership, he or she should quietly reach out to build a small team. To prepare for its role, the team should seek family business education to learn the scope of its challenges and possibilities and to develop a shared language and conviction.

If the business leader is the one feeling the need for a family constitution, he or she can provide guidance and recruit other family members to assume leadership positions. But it is important that the business leader take a supporting role rather than center stage when the process of writing the constitution begins. Developing the depth and breadth of family leadership matters more than the constitution itself.

Emphasize process over content

Hardly any research proves that certain family business policies are more effective than others. Different families will arrive at diverse answers to such questions as how to define family membership, who votes the shares, who can work in the business, how much to provide for family income and liquidity, and what are the criteria for selecting family representatives to the board.

As long as the family works out the answers together and approves them in the end, those policies will be well adapted to that particular family.

So the success of the family constitution will stem more from how strongly the family sanctions its policies than from what the rules actually say. And since the constitution cannot conceivably address all the policies the family will ever need, the family will have to call upon the skills it learned while drafting the constitution to add or revise policies when necessary. In fact, each step in the drafting process offers an opportunity to practice decision-making skills, including settling such logistical matters as when and where to meet, whether babies and cell phones are allowed in meetings, and how to develop agendas and enforce meeting preparation. Other skills, such as negotiating and conflict management, may need to be taught by an outside advisor, but families usually find these educational seminars to be a fun, bonding experience. Figure 9.2 illustrates the hierarchy of skills and training one third-generation family decided it needed to successfully draft its constitution.

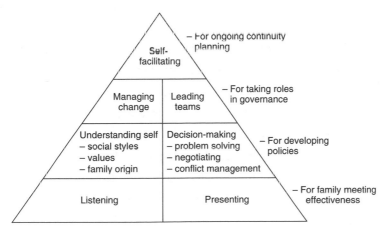

Figure 9.2 Family skills pyramid

Individuals have varying degrees of tolerance for process and open-ended assignments, and balancing dialogue with decisiveness is a delicate art, especially in families. To increase everyone's comfort level, each constitution drafting session should combine elements of fun, skills education, discussion, and, as important, completed tasks.

Create more than policies

In deciding to write a constitution, most families focus first on the policies that regulate family–business interaction and ownership rights and responsibilities. This orientation is natural when the motivation for a family constitution is to protect the business. Since ownership problems can wreak company havoc, families often make it a priority to revise an existing Owners' Contract or Shareholders' Agreement. Legal requirements shape the content so there is little demand on family members to be emotionally vulnerable.

A family that goes no further in its constitution than securing its ownership rights, however, runs two risks. First, if ever family relations are strained or an interpretation of a rule is needed, the family will hold win–lose debates rather than take a broader and more enlightened perspective on the disagreement. In those situations, the family would do well to step back and reflect on the values and principles described in its Family Philosophy. Solutions to problems often become much clearer when the family can articulate answers to such questions as: Why do we have this constitution? What is our collective purpose? What are the values and principles behind our policies? And when there is a dispute over a rule, a close reading of the Family

Philosophy will likely reveal the policy drafters' intent based on the values they espoused.

This defined set of values shared by the family becomes increasingly important the further removed descendants are from the founder and his or her passion for the business. The Family Philosophy serves as a moral beacon to successors who, all too often, tend to slip into practices common to public companies, such as maximizing shareholder value and stock price, instead of keeping alive the tenets of the family's businesslike patience to pursue long-term goals or maintaining stable ties with stakeholders.

The second risk of neglecting to include a Family Philosophy in a constitution is that spending family meeting time addressing only possible issues and rules is not much fun. The family may well lose its energy to continue the process.

The family constitution: a sum of three parts

The family constitutions of successful business-owning families include the following three agreements:

- *Shareholders' Agreement* – legal regulations affecting ownership rights and responsibilities.
- *Family Business Policies* – rules enforced by moral support of how the family and the business interact with each other. (Refer back to Figure 9.1.)
- *Family Philosophy* – the values and the principles the family holds important.

Few constitutions, however, include the Family Philosophy, even though it is the glue that binds families so they can find the strength to overcome future differences and the enthusiasm to face new challenges. The Family Philosophy incorporates the family's collective mission, the family's values, and the family's principles or beliefs that guide decisions.

The more attention paid to Family Philosophy and understanding what the family stands for, the easier it is to make difficult decisions and set policies on controversial issues. And the clearer those values and principles are, the more readily the family can amend or alter its policies to reflect the reality of changing circumstances or a new generation's insights. Ironically, it is the 'soft' elements of the family constitution that strengthen its durability and compliance.

Some families wisely invest the time and energy to attach to each policy a preamble that states the circumstances at the time a policy was established, the beliefs and principles behind each agreement, and the different perspectives and insights that were considered.

Assume no right answers

Many families seek reassurance from experts or from other families that the policies they set are correct.

While it is useful for families to study other constitution models, it is more important that the policies fit the particular family's business, ownership circumstances and culture. For example, the composition of the business's board depends, at least in part, on the ownership structure of the family. Precedent and the condition of the business will dictate the family's dividend policy. And decisions on employment practices may be a function of the international scope of the business or the sophistication of its managers. Cribbing from other constitutions will initially save time, but eventually the family will reject those policies as irrelevant and will have to invest the effort to create their own.

Decide how to decide

In their haste to put policies in place, families rarely consider in advance how they will vote to ratify their decisions. The conundrum is that families have to decide on the decision rule without a voting method in place. One solution is to ask the family leadership to determine how the family should ratify the constitution *before* any decisions come up for a vote.

Other families believe all decisions should be unanimous. This may work for small families comprised of members of the first and second generations. But as the family grows and encompasses several generations, it needs a democratic voting system that allows for some disagreement without allowing special interests to override proposed policies. Each component of the family constitution also requires different voting criteria for ratification. In addition, votes for Shareholders' Agreements are generally issued on a per-share basis while the Family Philosophy and the Family Business Policies are sanctioned by a one-person-one-vote system.

Figure 9.3 lists the preferred voting methods for small and large families.

	0–7 family members	8 or more
Vote on Family Philosophy	Unanimous	Super majority
Vote on Family Business Policies	Consensus	Majority
Vote on Shareholders' Agreement	Super majority	Super majority

Figure 9.3   Preferred voting methods

Look further afield for the values

Most families feel they are their own best experts on identifying their family's values. After all, who knows them better?

Undoubtedly the family will hit upon some shared values by asking each member to define the family ethos. But there are better, more objective ways to help identify and describe values that make them more distinct and meaningful to the family. A fun approach is for family members to relate favorite stories about the founder, revered relative, or the family history. Often specific values will emerge from the family's folklore.

Alternatively they could ask long-time friends or associates of the family to recount the distinguishing values of the family. Non-family managers or outside advisors to the business can often elucidate the family's most authentic principles based on the traits the company prizes in its employees, how the firm differs from other family businesses, and how the public perceives the company.

After receiving feedback from outside sources, one family reworded some of its values. 'Freedom' was replaced by 'trusting individual responsibility,' 'long-term commitment' became 'stewardship,' and 'integrity' gave way to 'honorable.' By substituting more nuanced values in its Family Philosophy, the family felt a stronger connection.

Values sanctioned by the entire family also provide the source of confidence the family needs to review and amend the constitution in the future. Even in small families where shared values are part of the collective consciousness, formalizing them in a Family Philosophy is the most reliable way to transmit them to future generations.

Tomorrow's constitution

When family constitutions are initiated in the wake of problems – as most are – the more aggrieved family members often overreact and push for draconian policies to quash any suggestion of the problem recurring. New generations, too, set their rules in response to the difficulties of their predecessors. One set of historical experiences becomes the evidence for natural laws of human nature.

Studying the evolution of more than 30 family constitutions showed that families who have experienced problems with individuals compromising the business's strength adopt constitutions that are very protective of the company. Rules are stricter, legally enforceable, and permanently fixed. Family leaders, for example, may insist on stringent qualifications for family members to work and progress in the firm. These requirements will not only make the family defensive, they may even dissuade bright young people from entering the business so that there are no successors.

At the other extreme, individuals who blame the business for alienating or splintering the family in the past will set policies that are family-friendly, informal, and easily changed – at the risk of predisposing family members to put their personal interests over the needs of the business.

Families, then, need to take measures to guard against allowing a painful history to inform future policy. As a first step, professional counseling may be necessary to heal old wounds and mend fractured family relations; the family constitution is not the vehicle for dealing with family dysfunction or past disputes.

And as the family reflects on its business history, it needs to be mindful of how biases can perpetuate expectations for conflict, resulting in unnecessarily strict policies. This openness and self-awareness will also foster increased trust and confidence among the family.

Families should also determine why their current primary allegiance is to the business or to the family. Usually each generation overreacts to the bias of the former generation. Eventually equilibrium is reached. The more the self-awareness, the sooner equilibrium is reached (see Figure 9.4).

Culture or experience will also cause families to favor certain attributes when setting policies, such as:

Flexibility   or   Stability
Individuality   or   Collectivity
Freedom   or   Unity
Values   or   Rules
Optimism   or   Pessimism

The family that recognizes how these orientations influence their decisions are less likely to create a family constitution that balances the past and the future.

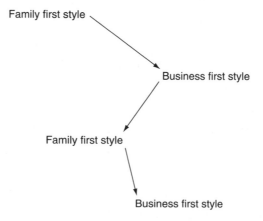

Figure 9.4   Transitions in family constitution approach

Flexibility provides stability

The idea of a family constitution carved in stone comforts business leaders worried about family interference in the business or family members too weary of the complex process of forging the constitution to contemplate revising it. Many constitutions, therefore, are written to last as long as national laws permit.

Contrary to popular belief, these long-lived, iron-clad constitutions hinder family stability rather than promote it. When circumstances inevitably change, the family will not have the experience or the time to adapt. Any change, therefore, becomes a hot issue, especially since the constitution's amendment rules are intentionally onerous. Gathering enough support to make revisions is nearly impossible with a requirement that approval must be near unanimous.

The constitution, designed for stability, instead puts a huge stress on the business and the family. Sometimes the only remedies are to dissolve the business or file suit against other family members.

Consider the family that creates a 10-year trust to enforce rigid rules of voting or distributions. The next time the family discusses the topic is just before the trust comes up for renewal. Under the pressure of a deadline, the family starts arguing about the purpose and usefulness of the trust, and individuals seize the opportunity to complain about every perceived injustice or slight by other family members. The family branches are not even close to reaching any agreement – certainly not unanimously.

Because the family has neglected to periodically review and amend its constitution, it cannot readily reinstate the continuity planning process when it is forced to do so. The family's decision-making and communication skills have atrophied from disuse, and the role of family leadership may also have been impeded.

Had the family adopted a flexible constitution, however, the matter of renewing a trust would not have created the rancorous conflict the family so desperately wanted to avoid. A better policy would have required the family to extend or revise the trust every three or five years to keep the family governance process fresh and to promptly address individuals' grievances before they had a chance to fester. And if a large issue arises, there is more time to resolve it.

Continuous review does not apply only to legal agreements. Rather than wait for a crisis or conflict to force a revision of a policy, many family leaders make it a point to review their entire constitutions annually to assess whether they meet the needs of the family and the business. Some families even place sunset provisions on their policies so that each generation will have to craft its own, thereby promoting younger family members' resolve and commitment to continuity.

An expanding family of several generations and in-laws will also have to update its Family Philosophy to reflect members' varied upbringings, education, and even countries of origin. One approach is to relax the details while adhering to the fundamentals. The value that all are of one faith, for example, may be replaced with the principle that all believe in God. Or commitment to family may be redefined as spending time with family rather than working 80-hour weeks in order to provide for family. In other cases, certain values may have to be deleted from the constitution. One founder whose motto was 'never trust anyone' created a business culture that encouraged personal fiefdoms among managers. His son, who inherited the business, was just as adamant that teamwork and trust were the cornerstones of success and gave each employee a piece of the toppled Berlin Wall to symbolize the new set of values that would be governing the company.

Building continuous review into the family constitution also reinforces the family's faith that they have the power to fix what does not work. A family accustomed to amending its constitution can comfortably correct a mistake in, say, its nominating process for family leadership. And nothing builds trust like a family pledge to continually monitor its processes for fairness to all. A family that is entrusted to preserve the currency of its constitution by continually renewing it becomes stronger, more united, and, ultimately, more stable.

Take the focus off the business

Ask a sampling of families why they have constitutions and the answer is remarkably consistent: to preserve the continuity of the family business. Their constitutions are all about the business: policies govern how the family affects the business; the constitution's preamble, mission, and philosophic underpinnings focus on keeping the business successful; and only those closest to the business find the document relevant to their lives.

Paradoxically, however, the less emphasis on protecting the business, the greater the likelihood the family will preserve it. If the family feels its constitution serves to sustain the continuity of the family by establishing distinct family leadership to look after family interests, individuals are more apt to place the common good – conserving the business – over their personal needs. For example, the constitution can establish a Family Council to maintain strong, healthy relations among family members so they can effectively make decisions about the business and carry out their objectives and mission. All family members directly benefit from the Family Council's activities, which can include coordinating social events to encourage family camaraderie, hosting workshops to build the skills the family needs to work as a team, and providing funding for individuals to pursue personal and professional enrichment. (See Figure 9.5 for a Family Council job description.)

Enterprising Families truly do put family first and their constitutions reflect that. The term 'Enterprising Family' refers to families with a collection of family interests – including a business – under the leadership of a family leadership function, such as a Family Council (Ward, 2003).

Here's how Enterprising Families operate. Together, the family members decide they will build other enterprises beyond the original family company, such as several new businesses, a private foundation for philanthropy, a family investment company, and a family office. All are governed by the

---

Meaning and purpose

- Family mission and vision
- Shared values
- Fun times
- Philanthropy
- Sense of history
- Ceremonies and traditions
- Opportunities to be involved and contribute

Education and development

- Interpersonal skills and competence
- Business and philanthropy understanding and leadership
- Personal development and mentoring
- Family life and parenting
- Social and professional networks

Leadership and decision-making

- Decision-making processes
- Succession and estate plans
- Policies defining family relationship with enterprises
- Code of behavior
- Governance instructions and bylaws
- Information and communications

Figure 9.5   Functions of the family council

family constitution and the Family Council. Now there are many more opportunities for family members to participate and contribute according to their talents and interests. And because family needs are being met through the entire enterprise, including sitting on the boards of the various entities, the companies can be run like businesses without the interference of unqualified family members who want to manage the operations. There is even more incentive for the businesses to be managed well, since they are the source of funding for the other family enterprises. The orientation is solidly family first, and worries about family continuity disappear as members take increasing pride in the new enterprise.

Conclusion

Family constitutions are a high priority for business-owning families. Very often, however, they are written for the wrong reasons, by the wrong people, in the wrong way. That is because the approach to drafting a successful constitution is counterintuitive to most people. Family members' strong desire to protect their business often causes them to overlook the equally important duty of safeguarding the continuity of the family. But when the constitution is created specifically to meet the goals of the family, the result is a stronger and enduring commitment by family to preserve the business.

The constitution must embrace family leadership independent of the business rather than merely govern how family interacts with the business. The more flexible the constitution, the more durable it is. And, above all, the experience of the family working together in a democratic process to draft the constitution will strengthen the family and its business much more

Positive:	The primary purpose is to perpetuate the family, not protect the business.
Philosophic:	Values and principles are set first to explain policy decisions.
Personal:	The document is particular to each family, not extracted from generic best practices.
Participate:	The process is broadly inclusive, not the work of a few or an advisor.
Process Over Project:	Attention and patience with the process is more important than speed or the content.
Paradoxical:	The constitution's resolve puts the family first *and* governs the business in the best interests of the business.

Figure 9.6   The six P's of successful family constitutions

than the document's content. The best constitutions follow no checklist of prescribed universal policies but are uniquely tailored to fit the particular family and its principles while serving to inspire idealism and enthusiasm for family and its business.

Figure 9.6 lists the attributes of constitutions common to families who believe that the welfare of the business and of the family are greatly enhanced by the existence of the other (Montemerlo and Ward, 2004).

References

Montemerlo, D. and Ward, J. 2004. 'How a formal family agreement can benefit your business.' *Families in Business*, September/October: 72–73.
Ward, J.L. 2003. 'The ultimate vision for continuity?' *Families in Business*, September/October: 78–79.

10

Good News for Family Firms: You Don't Have to Worry About the New Rules in Corporate Governance. But...

Ulrich Steger

For the most part, family businesses can ignore the plethora of new corporate governance regulations such as Sarbanes–Oxley or the Hicks Report since these so-called reforms do not require compliance from most private companies. However, this privilege lulls most family firms into complacency about governance. Family firms should use this freedom to look deeper at real, not legislated governance issues. Family companies share many of the same dilemmas as their non-family counterparts, plus some others that can be even more complicated and challenging.

Before examining some uncommon views of corporate governance, a little background on Sarbanes–Oxley is necessary. During the 'new economy' stock market bubble, most family businesses were, by definition, old economy. They were condemned to a sort of shadowy existence on the fringes of the new virtual business world. To hang around over generations was just not 'cool' and did not provide fees for investment bankers.

The bubble eventually burst and the 'day after' revealed the darker side of public market capitalism – greed. Greed misled and ripped off investors. Rogue investment practices at times even included fraud. That is not really new. Every market implosion since the 17th century Dutch tulip bubble, one of the earliest significant commercial disasters, has destroyed value. These catastrophes redistributed wealth to those who were early players but wiped out the savings of those who came late to the game. Such high-stakes diversions were followed by a 'moral hangover' when the party was over. This time, the 'new economy' bubble broke, investors lost trust, prosecutors discovered malfeasance and the media made sure that everyone knew.

The ensuing recession, which often follows a bubble, revealed what outsiders and auditors often chose to ignore when things were booming. The backlash was swift and severe. Regulators and politicians all over the world created new far-reaching rules. American regulators led with the Sarbanes–Oxley Act. The focus was corporate governance, a term barely used in public parlance five years ago. Even notorious laggards in stock market regulation, for example Greece, jumped on the bandwagon. The Parmalat case convinced even lukewarm continental European enthusiasts that corporate governance was not just an Anglo-Saxon affair.

The results of these efforts are visible. Just about every publicly quoted company now faces a barrage of new and complex regulations, stock market listing requirements, directors' fiduciary liability rules and voluminous codes of conduct, the latter often with the mandate 'comply or explain.' No wonder there is now such a renewed interest in private ownership.

The motivation to avoid the high costs of public ownership was never greater.

Is this good news for privately held family businesses? Yes. But, contrary to conventional wisdom, we would amend that answer to include '…and no.' The answer is yes because avoiding compliance costs of the new regulations is another source of competitive advantage. Corporate governance reforms routinely cost millions. Moreover, an often-overlooked consequence is the time and energy spent by CEOs and boards to ensure compliance – an expensive distraction.

The answer is also no, however, because it would be naive to ignore the fact that private family businesses also have corporate governance problems of their own. With no legal mandate requiring that owners address their own distinct issues, the impetus to embrace good governance practices may be absent. Most questions of corporate governance are universal. The answers, however, are specific. And without legal compliance as a benchmark, many private family companies may struggle to find effective answers for today's world.

The purpose of this chapter is not to repeat mainstream thinking and research. It would be a task in itself to sort out the gold nuggets from the rocks. Rather the goal is to provide some perhaps contrarian views, based on research at IMD. There are many commonly held myths that offer promise to such contrarian thinking.

The fit is everything

The first myth to tackle is the assumption that corporate governance regulations really drive the way a company behaves. Instead there are four situational factors that really mold business behavior (as explained below). The result is that there is no such thing as 'best practice' in corporate governance. What counts is the fit of the governance system to the specific company. The fit is what creates value.

For family firms the question of fit is even more complex. Conventional thinking has the board of directors as the central organization of business governance. With family companies there are other key players – the owners. The market's knee-jerk approach has been to establish complicated, legalistic and, consequently, rigid governance structures. But this tactic can prove especially harmful to family businesses. When fit is the key to value, and the business environment is dynamic, rigid rules or protocols designed to restrict flexibility attack the very strength of family-owned enterprises – the ability to adapt and to act rationally in their long-term best interest.

Factors shaping corporate governance practice

There is a strong belief held by regulators, academics and, curiously, the wider public that tighter regulation of corporations is necessary to drive new rules for corporate behavior. One question now being considered is whether one-tier or two-tier boards protect shareholders best. The first is typical for the Anglo-Saxon world and unites executive and non-executive members of the board in a single entity with ultimate responsibility for the company. Northern Europe is predominantly a two-tier system in which the leadership responsibility is divided between a non-executive supervisory board and an executive board of management.

The board of British Petroleum, for example, is legally a one-tier board, with an independent chairman and a majority of non-executive directors. In practice, these individuals act as though there is a two-tier structure – setting the 'space' in which the CEO and the top team can work independently, setting targets and evaluating performance, and debating major decisions that affect the future of the company.

In the German context, there have been examples where the non-executive chairman of the supervisory board effectively runs the company. This may not be in accordance with German law, but strong CEOs with a great track record tend not to let go easily when they retire and transition to the position of the chairman of the supervisory board.

Another example is the tendency in global companies for power to shift to executives. The more global a company, the more complex the business becomes. (According to IMD research, maintaining a global enterprise is the leading indicator of organizational complexity, more predictive than sheer size. In the 1970s, for example, American steel companies were huge, but nevertheless simpler operations than global businesses.) With this increased complexity, it is more and more difficult for a non-executive board member to understand all relevant risks, know different markets and assess investment opportunities. This inevitably shifts the balance of power toward the company's executives who are involved full-time, regardless of regulation and ownership. As information on strategic issues can be imprecise, even diffuse, top management often has abundant opportunities to present its action plan in the best light, without legally misleading the board.

What then are the most important factors shaping corporate governance practice, if not regulation? IMD research has identified four primary factors.

- *Personalities matter*: Whether regulators like it or not, effective CEOs inevitably shape the way the corporate governance system works. Through personal initiatives, leveraging influence and wielding individual power, the CEO dominates the interpretation of facts and designs the governance process, information allocation and timing. This can happen independent of whether a two-tier or one-tier board system prevails. If a strong personality combines with concentrated ownership, as in a family business, the leader may wield inordinate power.

- *Strategy/business model*: In different stages of the corporate life cycle and in different industries, different corporate governance systems are appropriate. A start-up in a volatile high-tech industry has different requirements (i.e., more coaching and risk management by the board) than a more mature business where the board needs leverage to fight complacency and bureaucracy. An aggressive growth strategy, based on mergers and acquisitions, would require different supervision than a more gradual, organic approach.

- *Business environment*: Not only the established rules and regulations are important, but also the unwritten 'do's and don'ts.' They can shape the political environment, social norms, traditions or public expectations. Families with high name recognition may face additional requirements, especially if they are private companies. A lack of mandated financial disclosure carries a burden to have at least as high hurdles for corporate governance as non-family publicly listed firms if the family brand is to be protected.

- *Ownership/capital markets*: Many previous and current governance rules have been driven by institutional investors who see themselves as representatives of a wider shareholder group. Private owners can shape appropriate governance practices even more fervently than fragmented owners of public companies.

Out of these briefly sketched issues, it is pretty clear that there is no 'best practice' or 'one size fits all' in corporate governance. This is, however, the implication of many codes of conduct. The needs of family businesses require a particularly tailored approach.

The role of the board in family business

With no 'best practices' to set the standard, the various roles the board plays and the various roles of outsiders in the governance system of the family business need to be examined. There are four different types of governance systems.

- CEO-centered model – often found in the USA where the role of the CEO and chairman of the board is combined. Here one person dominates the governance system and its decisions. As discussed earlier, the more global and complex a company, the more the power shifts to the executives and is centralized in the role of the CEO. Even in governance systems in which the management board is by law equal and bears a fiduciary responsibility, 'imperial CEOs' have developed.
- Checks-and-balances model – the current favorite of regulators and even investment bankers, who had previously favored the CEO-centered model. Most of the recent changes in regulation are intended to strengthen the role of the board and independent directors, in order to control and supervise management better.
- Consensus model – culturally ingrained in many Asian and northern European systems. It not only emphasizes harmony in the board but also harmony with the business environment and stakeholders.

- Owner-centered model – not only relevant for family business, but also private non-family companies. It is vital to understand the specific role owners play and the governance implications for family business.

IMD Professor John Ward has identified five categories of family firms (operating, governing, active, investing and passive), and building on this framework, we immediately see the specific implications for corporate governance.

- *Operating owner*: Management is wholly or partly dominated by the owning family. If legal requirements exist for corporate governance, they are minimal and roles are allocated within the family. The transaction costs are extremely low, as trust and informality drive the governance process. The danger lies in the possibility that key decisions may be effected without thorough examination.
- *Governing owner*: Often outside managers run day-to-day operations, but the family dominates the (supervisory) board, directing and controlling the business from there. Family likely not only selects the management team but also has the final say on any important business decisions. Their presence has a huge influence on strategy, portfolio mix, synergies, culture, risk-preferences, organization and performance measurement.
- *Active owner*: More elaborate governance structures are typical in this category, with the family constituting only a portion of the (supervisory) board. External trustees play a more important role, especially when there are minority shareholders. However, the owners set the standards and processes for governance, often based on a checks-and-balances model and designed to assure the continuity of business and leadership.
- *Investing or passive owners*: The involvement of the family in the business is often reduced to the collection of dividends. The company is run

by management and the board. However, the stability implied by continued family ownership could have important consequences for the business model and the core strategy.

These governance frameworks have important implications for the board. Figure 10.1 indicates the different options correlating with the level of involvement of the owners.

- Operating owners often have a 'Proxy Board' of friends and family. Given the deep involvement of the owners in day-to-day operations, no agency problem exists. If there is any meaningful role for outsiders, it lies in the objective evaluation of the team around the operating owners and the mediation of potential family conflicts. This does not mean that operating owners cannot benefit from outside advisors who really know the company – but few in this position are ready to listen.
- Governing owners depend on a good board, often referred to as a 'Scout Board.' The role of outsiders is to support owners with advice on industry

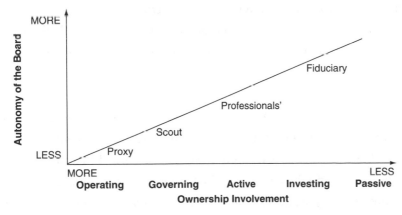

Figure 10.1   Board styles and owner involvement

trends, to challenge management on operational issues and to help evaluate management performance. External advisors can add valuable insight. Mitigation and reconciliation of conflicts are necessary as their occurrence is likely. Coordination between family governance and business governance becomes more and more crucial.

- Active owners depend even more on formal governance structures, especially as surviving family firms tend to be larger. Often families set the fundamental business values that the external board members must share in order to help operationalize them and support the corporate culture. Boards in this category need to be closely aligned with the owners while maintaining objectivity and independence – a 'Professionals' Board.' The synchronization of family and business governance at this stage is vital, as the power wielded by an individual family 'tribe' is often sufficiently large to cause trouble. External actors might find themselves in the unpleasant situation of protecting the business from family conflicts.

- Investing or passive owners do not differ much from non-family companies with the exception of strategy. Such uninvolved owners seek and need a 'Fiduciary Board.' Since a significant portion of individual wealth is tied up in an illiquid asset, risk-diversification is a more distinct concern for the family firm.

It should be noted that there is no natural progression to these categories. A family business in the sixth generation may still have operating owners, such as C&A. And, as the Ford Motor Company illustrates, even an investing family might again be called upon to act as operating owners. Therefore, it is important to look not for 'best practices,' but rather to seek the best fit.

Additional requirements for governance in the family business

Style of the board notwithstanding, the family business has to meet the general imperatives of good, context-sensitive corporate governance rules:

- Clear allocation of duties, responsibilities, power and accountability – especially the division of labor between board and top management, regardless of whether management ranks are occupied by family or not;
- Transparency in the business model/strategy, the planned and achieved results and the opportunity/risk preferences;
- Monitoring and compliance, supported by appropriate and rigorous follow-up;
- Professional qualifications and leadership competencies of the directors in line with the industry.

Particularly with regard to performance requirements, there can be no 'discount.' Family businesses must meet the same hurdles for competence and leadership skills as others in the industry. If this standard is not met, declining competitiveness will soon follow.

In a non-family company, every board member has equal rights and standing. Owner members on private family business boards cannot realistically be regarded as equal to non-family board members. This inequality does not mean that arguments from outside board members should be ignored. In every debate, analysis, or evaluation of options, each viewpoint should stand on its own merits, without regard for its advocate. However, it should be clear to everyone that the owners have the final say. In principle, this is the same for a publicly quoted company, but given the fragmented ownership, it is nearly impossible for owners to express a common will. One of the dilemmas in the governance of public companies is that the owners are practically unrepresented. When institutional investors step in, a new agency problem emerges. The managers of these funds have their own interests, which might not be the same as those of the broad class of shareholders. So, responsible ownership should be regarded as good news, even if it leads to some inequality.

All involved in the governance system of a family business have to understand the specific context and what is expected. As described above, depending on the level of ownership involvement, boards play different roles as long as transparency and a mutual understanding of the rules prevail. As no one is obliged to serve on family business boards, such a differentiation should not be an obstacle.

When owner-directors have more power, they also have more responsibility. One of the fundamental obligations of ownership is to set the values and basic rules for the business, as long as they are in conformity with local laws. With values and their impact on norms and cultural attitudes, the board then shapes the life of the company through strategic decision-making. An excellent example of strongly held beliefs and philosophy can be found in the following abridged version of the values statement of Lehmann & Voss, a fourth-generation Hamburg family business.

Lehmann & Voss & Co.

Our Values, Our Guidelines

Our Values
or: what counts for us

As a family business we think and plan long-term. And all of us are responsible for insuring that this finds expression in our daily activities. *That makes us predictable.*

The relationship between our managers and our employees is one of trust, as is that between those responsible for the market and our clients and suppliers. We stand by our word. *That makes us reliable.*

Our company is happy to incorporate change in order to remain successful. Yet we always hold to our course: our fixed points are mutual respect and a sound, socially-oriented entreprenurial spirit. *That makes us credible.*

Our Guideline
or: who we are and what we want

1. Our Company
As a chemicals company we aim to increase the value of our enterprise without taking dangerous risks or neglecting social and ecological factors. *That makes our activities sustainable.*

2. Our Strategy
We pursue three business strands: own production, distribution and trade. Our products and our service are of the highest quality, but there is always room for improvement. We seek the new mainly by developing the tried-and-tested. We are consequently growing our international involvement. *That makes us competitive.*

3. Our Clients

We work closely with our clients. Together with them we seek improvements and solutions to problems on a basis of trust and respect. *That makes us successful.*

4. Our Employees

Our dedicated employees participate in the company's economic success. The company offers them secure work places and satisfying working conditions and tasks. We prefer direct discussions, as we see problems as opportunities and not a reason for criticism. Our employees work in a responsible and results-oriented way.

That makes us socially responsible and appealing.

5. Our Managers

Our managers have sufficient scope for their own initiatives and decisions, and bear responsibility for the results in their respective sectors. They have a model function, giving encouragement while also making demands. Women and men have the same chances of promotion.

That makes managing in our company an ambitious and varied task.

To achieve the objectives behind our guideline, all of us must make our contribution in our respective fields.

At the end of a working week, we should be able to be proud of what we have achieved.

That makes Lehmann & Voss & Co. a special company.

Those who work in the governance system of a family business must share the organization's fundamental values. This does not preclude professional disagreements or differences of opinion. On the contrary, on this foundation of mutual understanding, issues and strategy can be debated even more rigorously. Principles can be more important than personalities in boardroom discussions. Beware, though. These shared values must not lead to 'group think,' which can be a breeding ground for complacency and tolerance of low performance. Family business boards need to guard against such 'group think' by seeking independent and family directors who bring disparate points of view and have the courage to express them.

The law of unintended consequences

There is one fundamental, but self-inflicted flaw in family business governance, both in the family and business dimension. Dominant, successful personalities in the family constellation can lead to a rigid dynamic that threatens the governance system. In non-family firms, lawmakers and regulators can mandate governance systems that adapt to changing circumstances. In a family business, the way out of ingrained practices can be profoundly more difficult.

A typical example can be found in the serious governance challenges faced by the third-generation Bata Shoe Organization of Canada. The patriarch intended to make the business immortal by setting up a trust and protecting it from the family. The trust did not prevent family conflicts, nor did the trustees prove to be vigilant guardians of the family's heritage. They presided over a declining business for far too long.

The happy ending of the Bata drama[1]

Hollywood could not have invented a better story of family and business struggle than that faced by the Bata Shoe Organization following World War II. Uncle and nephew battled for decades to determine who would control the company. The son quit as CEO. But it took hard work, persistence and dedication to straighten out this corporate governance challenge.

Founded in 1894 in Zlin, Czechoslovakia, the Bata Shoe Organization was set to become the largest global shoe manufacturer despite the turmoil of two world wars. However, the founder, Tomas Bata, left no will when he died in 1932, but instead a 'moral testament.' To make the company immortal and to ensure its future as a source of social benefits, he dedicated its shares to a public trust. But one paragraph could be interpreted as giving ownership control to his half-brother Jan, not to his then 17-year-old son, Thomas J. Bata. The situation did not immediately cause trouble, as Thomas J. was still young and not yet ready to take up the reins of such a vast enterprise. However, after World War II, when Thomas J. was grown up and ready to assume his rightful role in the company, Jan refused to cede control. It took a legal battle that lasted for nearly two decades for Thomas to regain ownership. His persuasion and sheer will led executives in the company's nearly 30 local subsidiaries to embrace him as their leader.

---

[1] For a full account, see the following IMD cases: IMD-3-1084 and IMD-3-1085.

His son, Thomas G. Bata Jr., faced another dilemma in the late 1980s. Well-meaning, but aged trustees watched over a decade of decline in the company which was then structured as self-perpetuating trusts. The trustees supervised the destruction of more than half of the family's wealth – and very nearly the Bata reputation. It took almost another decade of contentious wrangling for Thomas G. Bata Jr., together with his sisters, to develop a corporate governance structure that established clear accountability and responsiveness to the rapidly changing world of a globalizing consumer business.

The dedication of the Bata family to its heritage and the integrity of the family name resulted in a long fight to regain control of the company. The four third generation siblings developed and staged a turnaround. Things could easily have been worse.

The Bata case is not an atypical example. It is sad that future realities are seldom foreseen in the will or contract. Given the many potential issues, it is not difficult to miss at least one. Nor do provisions always work out as intended. People change over time and what works at one time may not work under different circumstances. Promising young heirs can take unexpected turns, turbulence in the business may require rare turnaround skills, tax rules can change, profitable business models may disappear when knowledge cannot be protected. The list of examples that trigger serious reconsideration of important governance rules is nearly unlimited.

So, what can be done? Three recommendations can help: first, a 'sunset' clause should be the basis of the family and business governance systems;

second, focus on a few basic rules to ensure the continuity of core values; finally, include conflict resolution rules.

The first idea is that each responsible generation gives to the next generation a new governance system for the family and the business. It is part of their duty. It should reflect changing circumstances like the growth of the family or the business, foreseeable trends such as industry consolidation and experience gained including selection criteria for family representatives on boards and managing conflicts of interest.

Second, instead of trying to foresee every possible situation, the basic agreement should lay out the core values of the family and the business. Company policies must necessarily follow from these core values. For example, if the goal is to stay independent, then the sales of shares/ property rights must be restricted and tightly controlled by the family office.

Third, arbitration rules must be in place in case of conflicts in the family or business and to provide for necessary adaptation of the governance system over time. Historically, the family is the primary source of contentious debate. In the business sphere, the rules for conflict resolution are generally much clearer and often anticipated. Disagreements are not necessarily bad. Innovation cannot be born without conflict. Divergent viewpoints are legitimately shaped by different perspectives. Those who run the family business are often more ready to invest in new ventures than those who simply want to enjoy the benefits of a steady, robust cash flow. The issue then is adopting a fair process to resolve these differences. In the past, conflict resolution was frequently the purview of the 'family elder' who considered each argument and then rendered a decision.

The decline of patriarchal structures in families makes conflicts within the family more likely. No one really has the power to discipline dissenters.

Therefore, either court cases are pursued (mostly an unpleasant experience, dividing the family further) or neutral parties are selected to mediate and resolve crises. To be effective, trusted outsiders must be appointed *before* any conflict arises. Many families do not like people outside the family deciding their destiny. But this reticence could increase the pressure to find a solution within the family first. The difficulty in finding external people who know the family and the business yet are not tied to any of the 'family tribes,' could bring the warring factions together.

Outlook: where does the value added come from?

It is conventional wisdom that dedicated and responsible ownership considerably lowers transaction costs. However, the way ownership rights and responsibility are exercised in varying contexts differs widely. The identification of a value-added governance system has to be more specific and based on the merits of the individual situation and the closeness of fit in serving the family and business most effectively.

There is one case in which the family as owner can always add value – the transparency and continuity of core business values. Formal and informal corporate policies are derived from these values. The litmus test for the effectiveness of family owners is therefore the readiness and the competence with which they provide a clear set of principles that guide the life of the operation. This differs from the 'motherhood and apple pie' vision and mission statements in most non-family companies, which triggers cynicism and the disinclination to espouse stated values.

Selecting independent directors

As discussed earlier, despite the fact that in some instances family members may assume primary managerial and supervisory responsibility, external professionals need to be involved in the family firm. The best way to incorporate fresh, objective viewpoints into this process is to ensure that strong, competent outside professionals hold seats on the company board. The board bears ultimate responsibility for the long-term direction of an enterprise and so is in a position to play a crucial role. In family businesses, board members can contribute in another important realm. They are also custodians of the family's basic values that ultimately shape corporate culture and the way the firm conducts itself. This is not a trivial issue but it is one that has implications for the board recruitment process.

Gone are the days when the typical board was comprised of the CEO, hand-picked friends and two members amenable to the local community. Frantic efforts have begun to beef up boards with truly independent directors. Many companies have employed headhunters for this purpose, with mixed results. The use of headhunters also puts confidentiality at risk. Such high-level and important searches can take an extended period as management seeks to be sure of its choice. After all, there is no definitive test for potential board members and headhunters often have difficulty fully understanding the values dimension inherent in the family enterprise. In the past, there were often far more suitable candidates available than vacant board seats, which made things somewhat easier. But the situation has now reversed.

There is a more practical way to approach this issue. One has to admit that personal choices are subjective and the higher one moves up in the hierarchy, the more personal it can get. But two things can help – the transparency of the process and clarity of selection criteria. The latter includes not only the core values set by the family, but also a kind of job description.

In today's complex world, no one person possesses all requisite skills for successful board functioning. Excellent performance by a board requires a group effort and the composition of the team is vital. Who will complement existing competencies best? Are industry experts who are operational, battle hardened 'old hands' best, or someone who can liaise especially well with the family? It is important that the board and family ownership agree unanimously on what is needed.

The temptation for family firms is to see the criteria for an effective director as common to all businesses. It is not. The family business seeks directors who have two seemingly contradictory qualities: they remain faithful to values and principles and they challenge fundamental strategic assumptions and performance standards. Special instruction or heed is needed if a search firm is used to be sure this dilemma is well understood and addressed.

The board chairman has a pivotal role. Even if there is a Nominating Committee, the chairman must be involved and, without dominating the process, play two essential roles. First, the chairman must strike the balance between director empathy for the family's values and the director's capacity to constructively challenge management's *and ownership's* current thinking. And the chairman must assure that the family owners present clear values and expectations to the board.

It is unconventional to imagine independent directors as resources and critics to owners, in addition to their customary role as resources and critics to management.

Conclusion

Recent corporate scandals have brought increasingly rigid standards for corporate governance. Family-controlled firms have the privilege to examine those standards and to adopt a governance form suitable to their situation. That opportunity is very valuable as governance that fits the circumstances is surely preferable.

For all companies, the proper form of governance varies with the complexity of the company and the personality of the leader. Government and market laws make acknowledging those differences very difficult. Therefore, family companies have a competitive advantage in governance.

But family owners also have a greater responsibility. They must resist the conventional wisdoms of how the board functions and what to look for in independent directors. Instead, they must take the time and care to design their governance system.

Further, the owners have the challenge to clarify and assert their values as the core of how the business is conducted and what the directors oversee. Yet, with the more powerful force of values, encouraging vigorous debate on strategic issues in the boardroom is both more possible and more difficult. It is more difficult to avoid 'group think.' To overcome that risk the chairman requires special skills, as do the independent board members.

On the other hand, when core values are the foundation of the governance system, the quality of debate and the conviction to achieve is ever greater. Happily, family firms do not have to follow all the new rules in corporate governance. Instead, they can govern in a way most appropriate to the circumstances in their company. This is the counterintuitive truth: the value from governance comes not from the necessary compliance, but from the fit.

11

The Value of Hands-On Ownership

John L. Ward

The conventional view of the stodgy family business is being overturned as more and more studies reveal that family businesses outperform other businesses and achieve greater longevity. Researchers want to know how family companies achieve better performance and why. Many believe that their higher performance and greater longevity are related, and that family businesses must be better adapted to compete in some way. Researchers are looking for the source of this competitive advantage.

This chapter will explore a new theory about the role of concentrated ownership in supporting business performance, and explore ways to increase the potential benefits of concentrated ownership over time. This theory holds that the small, distinct ownership groups of family businesses are what distinguish them from other businesses. Family ownership groups are capable of maintaining concentrated control and linking ownership and business goals directly and personally. Family members are often present in management and the boardroom, facilitating many important decisions.

Family ties serve to keep ownership better informed and to support more direct communication between the family and business. This results in building mutual understanding and trust.

The ability to develop and maintain trust across the business system is the special competency families bring to business. Trust is based on good communication and one-on-one relationships. Families create webs of communication and relationships that link directly to individuals. These networks serve to both flow information out, and bring feedback back in. This two-way communication is an important dynamic, which assures the alignment of ownership and business purpose in decision-making. Family networks can foster a higher degree of trust, which enables a higher degree of strategic consistency, and patience. According to this theory, concentrated ownership provides a distinct competitive advantage, and sustaining ownership engagement is the key to optimizing business performance.

This theory runs counter to a common view in family business, which argues that it is best to build a firewall between the family and the business. Many family businesses try to keep non-employed family shareholders deliberately apart from the business and its managers. This view holds that most family owners are not well informed enough to add value, and that their engagement only leads to meddling. According to this way of thinking, the interference of family owners not only distracts management, but it often chases the best managers away. While this can occur, it is not an inevitable outcome.

These negative assumptions lead to the wrong conclusions about the potential for informed ownership to add value. Family businesses that work with their family ownership groups enjoy the greatest competitive advantages. Actively engaging with ownership and educating them about the business helps to define the proper roles and responsibilities of owners. The other strategy of building walls between ownership and the company nearly always backfires eventually. An issue arises, the owners awaken and become angry, then overstep their proper roles within the system.

In essence, the more owners are drawn in, the more they will understand and accept the boundaries of their roles. When this understanding is combined with a close ownership link to the board, the most effective governance is created. This, in turn, assures that the management team has clear objectives and support for achieving them. When roles are clear and there is communication across the entire family business system, then it is possible to leverage the competitive advantage of concentrated control and achieve optimal business performance.

Sometimes inactive family owners believe that dedicated family managers deserve their trust, and conclude they should provide them with 'blind trust.' Some people believe this unquestioning trust is a great strength of family business, but not so. Blind trust does not hold up under the stress of the difficult and contested decisions that inevitably arise in family business. This is particularly true when the financial stakes of key decisions are quite high to individuals, as is often the case in concentrated family ownership. Family owners rarely all agree, and the ability to express reasoned dissent is critical to maintaining trust. Family managers and their boards should prefer ownership trust built on knowledge and informed consent (and dissent), over trust based solely on personal loyalty.

One of the other liabilities of blind trust is that it can make family managers inappropriately risk-averse. Family managers who receive blind trust can begin to feel a tremendous responsibility to individual family owners. They can feel overly pressured to avoid conflict or to preserve the family's wealth and reputation, and become so cautious that they are unable to pursue appropriate levels of business risk. On the other hand, when the family managers have the informed support of shareholders, they can take wise, strategic risks that they might otherwise avoid. Maintaining concentrated and informed ownership is often critical to the family business's ability to take unconventional risks and actively pursue strategic advantage.

The theoretical foundation

Chapter 2 explored the theory that family companies pursue unconventional strategies. It explained how strategic agility and adaptability allowed family businesses to create and capture more value. The theory presented here argues that patient and informed ownership is required to successfully pursue unusual strategies. The most successful families maintain their concentrated ownership control and focus on supporting the creation of distinct, competitive advantages within the business.

Family owners typically hold a large financial stake in their company, and tie up most of their personal net worth with the future of the business. Because of this, family owners pay very close attention to financial performance and strategy. They know their companies and industries well and will patiently support unconventional strategies that provide more promise for the long term. Often, family companies create, and retain value, reinvesting over long periods of time. Taxation issues can reinforce this tendency. Transfer of retained capital to succeeding generations is often perceived as more advantageous to the family and business than extraction of capital. This leads to the patient cultivation of financial resources in the form of business assets.

Business assets tend to be relatively illiquid, and most investors would not accept the inherent risk of concentrating wealth in a single illiquid asset. Most would not accept a time horizon stretching to their children and grandchildren, either, but this is precisely the nature of family owners. Their commitment often involves a sense of mutual identity between the family and the business. The family and business share a history, sometimes share a name, and a sense of family pride often underpins a legacy view of the business. All this supports the unusual level of financial commitment found in family ownership groups.

More and more, research is showing that this commitment to retaining business assets coupled with strategic patience really pays off. The challenge, then, becomes maintaining this enabling relationship over time. As families and their businesses grow and change, new approaches are necessary to sustain this symbiotic combination. Cultivating and renewing trust is the key to sustaining an enabling ownership/business relationship. This is particularly true with each generational transition, and trust within the family is as important as trust between owners and managers. An active, ongoing process of ownership engagement is vital to creating trust, and this is particularly true in periods of ownership and management successions, or in strategic transitions.

The nature of business is change, and families that actively cultivate trust can more readily handle the stress and uncertainty of change. Family ownership groups also accumulated knowledge from their long experience, which can help them handle periods of stress better. Their shared history often holds lessons about market cycles, and the long-term financial results that come with ownership patience and good management. The families that are most successful over the longest periods of time address the challenges of business change directly. They do this by actively and continuously renewing the ownership/management relationship through good governance.

Governance defines the responsibilities, relationships and roles of owners, directors and managers. Good governance is well adapted to both the needs of the business and the family, and will evolve in response to the changing requirements of the family or the business. Maintaining clarity about ownership's roles and responsibilities is a critical part of good family business governance, particularly as governance evolves over time. Ownership, the board, and management all need a shared understanding of their roles within the governance system, and they must remain effectively linked and mutually informed. The critical role of ownership is to promote clarity about the family's values, vision, and financial goals. To remain effective, governance must serve to foster communication that enables the creation of common goals and expectations, and serves to build shared trust.

In family business, good governance coupled with good business performance creates and sustains a foundation of trust. When there is trust across the system, management can propose the optimal long-term strategy, even if it is unconventional. If ownership is committed and patient, then the board can approve this optimal strategy, even if results may be slower to materialize. As part of this process, ownership needs to clearly define its expectations for future risk, return, payouts, and liquidity. All these components of the basic shareholder value proposition should be reflected directly in the strategy. Good governance provides for ongoing dialogue as strategies are executed over time, creating a continuous reassessment of the trade-off between maximizing short-term results and pursuing the highest long-term returns.

When ownership and management maintain a close tie through good governance, ownership has a better understanding of real market conditions and business performance. This allows ownership to develop a more accurate assessment of strategy and financial performance, and helps create clear expectations for management performance in good times and bad.

Active owners develop a more accurate view of the track record of the business and its managers, which helps support trust. Likewise, managers also develop a higher degree of trust in ownership, when they see a commitment to real understanding of the business. Sharing a common understanding of objectives and performance is the key to creating accountability and building trust in the family business.

Developing competence in both ownership and management is the key to enabling the family business strategic advantage. When knowledgeable ownership is combined with good management performance, this creates confidence, trust, and patience. This foundation supports ownership's ongoing commitment to long-term business strategies, and this commitment, in turn, enables management to actively pursue optimizing the business through advantageous, unconventional strategies. This train of thought leads to new insights on how to govern and lead a family business.

The model of family successions

Families in business tend to evolve with each generation succession. The first generation is usually embodied in a founder, who is often an entrepreneur. This single owner/manager concentrates power and defines the initial relationship of the family and the business. Founders often bring in family successors and transition to a family partnership, which can include their siblings, their spouse, and/or their children. Founders are notorious for holding onto control in the early stages of family partnerships, and transitions of authority are often delayed. Formal succession in both ownership and management is usually necessary before a true family partnership can wrest control. Most often, this takes the form of a sibling partnership in the second generation.

This first generational transition in family business is often the most critical. At this stage, roles and responsibilities usually begin to separate. Some siblings may be in the business and others may not. They may all share ownership equally, or sometimes active siblings are given a controlling stake. Founders usually make these decisions, and their actions tend to be guided by a desire to recreate concentrated control. Founders often have a hard time understanding how a partnership of family members can achieve effective control. Sometimes they create ownership vehicles to hold control, or prefer to pick a single, family successor, and delay the transition to a partnership. Eventually, however, most family businesses make the transition to shared ownership and active, family partnerships. The structures that emerge from this transition, whenever it happens, are usually the result of succession planning by a controlling owner/ manager.

These early structures are often based on pragmatic succession decisions. These decisions relate to the perceived needs and capabilities of the family and the business, as well as the founder's underlying values about fairness in the family. Once the founder is gone, the family must figure out how to make these inherited structures work. The key to this is managing the differentiation of roles, responsibilities, and authority created by the structure. At this stage, the family must figure out how to work as a team in a true partnership, both inside and outside the business. Often, this means differentiating family roles within ownership and management, but still finding ways to keep them linked.

As the family grows over succeeding generations, a number of different types of family owners can be identified by their roles. For example, operating owners work in the business, and governing owners serve in governance. Within the greater pool of family shareholders, there are three different types of owners – active, investing, and passive. Active owners remain knowledgeable about the business and are committed to engagement and communication. Investing owners are primarily concerned with financial performance, and passive owners take little interest in anything but dividends. As the family ownership group expands, it becomes increasingly challenging to cultivate active ownership that is willing to learn about the business, provide feedback to the system, and support the competitive advantages of the business.

As the family grows and structures evolve, individuals come to play multiple roles within the system. Active family members must increasingly know what hat they are wearing, and family culture must adapt to multiple roles with different levels of authority. Often, a key challenge is finding ways to share leadership effectively and create accountability. Equally important is cultivating an active connection between family owners who are inside and outside of the business, and enabling ongoing, two-way communication. Maintaining this active connection and assuring mutual ownership and management accountability becomes increasingly important as family roles begin to differentiate. Being clear about who has authority and how decisions are made becomes increasingly critical, particularly as governance structures become more complex.

These challenges are compounded when family successions lead to a collaboration of cousins. As the family increases in size, ownership becomes more dispersed and family roles vary even more widely. Generally, family employment levels tend to decrease, and the involvement of non-family managers in leadership increases. The business often develops more standard professional policies, structures, and practices. Simultaneously, each generational succession in ownership creates a family shareholder base that is ever larger and more removed from the business. As the business becomes more professional, an expanding ownership family faces the challenge of cultivating active ownership that is capable of effectively supporting the business.

As the family grows, it must continue to deal with the same issues – role separation, ongoing ownership/management communication, and resolving questions of authority and accountability. Increasingly, these issues are resolved on a system level, through the ongoing development of better governance practices. Maintaining the link between owners and managers becomes increasingly challenging with each generation succession, and requires a proactive adaptation of governance. Governance is where the family/business relationship occurs. Most often, governance evolves in relation to the needs of business, but in order to maintain concentrated ownership control, attention must also be given to the development of family governance.

Personal relationships and good communication are critical at all stages of family business evolution, but they are increasingly important as ownership disperses. Family relationships lubricate decisions and enable responsive change. This can become essential when complex governance adaptations are necessary at later stages of family and business development. When the family grows quite large, family governance is often the key to cultivating an effective family network and making the family business system work. Changes in governance practice are culturally challenging, and can be difficult for large families or their businesses to assimilate. But those families that successfully adapt governance at these later stages are capable of sustaining the concentrated ownership control that enables the family business competitive advantage.

The special role of the board of directors

In best practice, the board of directors is the center of business governance. The board is the ultimate legal fiduciary of the business, and must have the necessary authority to safeguard that responsibility. In family business, the board also serves to balance the requirements of the business and its ownership to keep the system functioning optimally. Public companies' boards are usually composed of a majority of independent directors, who represent the interests of dispersed shareholders and provide active oversight of management. In family companies, board composition varies widely, but most family business boards include family directors, who bring an ownership perspective directly into the boardroom.

In the early stages of family business development, founder owner/managers often hold control. At the founder stage, many businesses have no board or the board is only a legal entity with little authority. Founders tend to hold onto control, and use boards reluctantly. Some founders make use of advisory boards and a few will even create the independent boards of best practice. Board development at this stage is often driven by the founder's perceptions of the needs of the business, but it can also be influenced by the founder's perceptions of family capabilities. The use of advisory boards can be quite helpful to founders, who often need prodding to confront key issues like succession. Founders that establish independent boards often do so to insulate the business from the family.

Most often, the boards of family companies become active in the second generation, when a partnership of siblings develops. The board at this stage is often informal, functioning more as a board of the family than of the business. Informal sibling and cousin boards commonly become the place where ownership discussions occur. Often, family members from inside and outside the business participate and discuss business issues from an owner-ship perspective. While not performing the active oversight typical of a business board, these informal family boards can be highly involved in critical decisions about management succession, capital investment, and business strategy. Informal board practice continues for long periods of time in some families, often focusing exclusively on ownership decisions while leaving oversight of management to family business leaders. This simplifi-cation of governance can be cost-saving and quite effective at generating ownership consensus.

Informal governance does have limitations, however, and eventually growth in the business and the family will create a need for more developed practice. As the business grows, the need for active board oversight of management increases. As ownership disperses, the equity stake held by management tends to decline. As controlling interests move out of manage-ment, the fiduciary role of the board becomes more important. Families often resist changes to board practice because they are perceived as over-throwing family culture and tradition. Change raises issues around what the board does, how it does it, and who sits at the table. Managers tend to resist oversight, and family members want a seat at the table. Changing board practices can be disruptive, which is why informal practice lasts so long in many family companies.

Family businesses at all stages of development can benefit from formal board practice that includes independent directors. At the founder stage, a good board can help facilitate succession planning and next-generation career development. Early on, a good board helps the family capture and transmit its idiosyncratic business knowledge. Independent directors bring an outside business perspective and often provide fresh insights into the business. Their experience can help direct the organizational development of the business to take it to the next level. Good boards also take an active role in the development of planning processes, pushing management to develop appropriate strategic planning, and creating board-level capital investment strategies.

In family business, the objectivity of independent directors is especially valuable in capital investment decisions and setting the yardsticks for measuring performance. This can be particularly true when divestment or acquisition decisions are made, and an impartial assessment of business unit potential is required. Objectivity is often difficult for managers or family members to achieve. Ultimately, mature boards with independent directors can serve to assure a balance between the strategy of the company and the goals of family ownership. To accomplish this, the board must take on a special role in communications, and foster understanding and alignment of expectations across the family business.

Mature family businesses need boards that remain actively engaged with family ownership. There are many approaches to maintaining a close ownership/board relationship, and independent directors can play a special role in this process. Holding family and business meetings in sequence is a common practice, with family meetings first, so that family issues are resolved outside the boardroom. The ongoing exchange of meeting minutes and agendas is another common practice. Having directors attend some family meetings, or providing for family members to observe board meetings, are two recommended methods. Conducting a periodic joint assessment is also a good practice that provides for mutual perspective and feedback.

Fireside chats and other informal exchanges of information and views are another way that owners and directors can stay connected. Some families have programs for director mentoring or junior boards to support the development of individual governance participants. Independent directors can be very useful in these roles, and they can also serve as 'sounding boards' for disgruntled shareholders. While a sensitive task, inside directors can help draw the line between family and business issues, and send issues back to the family when appropriate. They can also help resolve disputes by representing the interests of all stakeholders and holding board decisions to the highest professional standards. While independent directors can help families reach compromise, they should recognize their limited role in the delicate process of managing family conflicts.

A good board is essential to maintaining the family business advantage over time. The boards of family companies resolve almost all the key issues faced by the business. To be effective, a board must assess the impact of decisions on the family, the management team, and the business. Good boards recognize when and how decisions stress the family business, and they actively seek to renew coherency. Conflict in family business systems often creates indecision, and boards must remain capable of decisive action. At the same time, they should recognize that making final decisions before adequate deliberation can intensify conflict. Creating openness and communication before decisions are made is often the key to a successful governance process. A good board will also address issues directly and transparently, promoting the hard work of decision-making and reconciliation. This effort must include both management and the family ownership.

As the final decision-maker, the board of a family company has a special role to play to governance. It must rise to the challenges of maintaining coherency and alignment between the ownership and its business. Good boards give attention to informing the family, and supporting active ownership consultation processes. Ownership feedback is essential to making effective, stable decisions. Good governance is required to renew and maintain the family business advantage over time. The board of directors is uniquely positioned to enable the communication and alignment that promotes the most effective governance.

The development of family governance

Family governance is unique to family businesses. Family governance can take many forms and tends to evolve over time. Its structures can include voting trusts, family and ownership councils, foundations, and family offices. All of these structures support family and ownership functions and sometimes they relate back to the board and the business. Voting trusts, foundations, and councils are often involved in nominating and electing directors, and they sometimes control the composition of the board. Family and ownership councils are usually the primary vehicles for communication and consultation with the board and business. Family offices often manage extracted wealth, but families with operating businesses also use family offices to support family governance. This can include planning and financial support for all aspects of family governance, as well as the development of governing family members, including family directors.

As family businesses mature, they tend to develop parallel family and business governance. As scale changes, the needs of the family and business become increasingly distinct, and separate structures are created to address the different functions related to these needs. While separate, these parallel governance structures must also interrelate. To be most effective, family and business governance must be actively linked and aligned. The development of parallel governance is unique to family business, and no two systems are exactly alike. Many are the result of historic decisions and reflect cultural traditions based on past practices. Governance tends to evolve organically, accumulating over time, as the family and business adapt to changing functional needs. Family businesses have only recently begun to understand parallel family business governance and how to proactively pursue its best practices.

The earliest forms of family governance are often trusts or other holding vehicles. These ownership structures are often created in response to tax planning and a desire to maintain consolidated voting control. Many highly successful families find that transfer taxes threaten their ability to pass down control of the business. When the value of the company grows too rapidly, transferring its ownership to the next generation can require extracting significant capital for taxes. The extraction of capital in generational transitions raises the cost of capital and can impact the business. As a result, many families create ownership trusts that continue over very long periods of time (some to perpetuity). These allow the family to shelter multiple ownership transitions from transfer taxes, keep value in the business, and build capital most efficiently over time.

Often, ownership is held collectively to maintain concentrated voting control. Most ownership vehicles are structured to maintain unified control, while sharing economic benefit across the family. Sometimes beneficial interest and voting control are held in separate trusts, so that the value of voting control can be minimized and maintained without severe tax consequences. This splitting of interests is common in complex trusts. Beneficial trusts can become quite large and complex over time, sharing economic benefits across an ever-increasing number of family members. Splitting trusts allows for this growth, while still maintaining separate, concentrated business control. This strategy is executed in many different ways, but most often takes the form of voting control held in a separate trust, whose trustees elect a majority of the board.

Governing complex trusts can become burdensome over time, and serving the needs of beneficial trusts can require a lot of professional support. Some families' needs become so great that they create their own trust companies or family offices. One advantage of collective ownership in trusts is that they can provide independent funding to support family functions. This enables the development of family offices, which can support the management of collective wealth and family governance. Maintaining family governance is often a primary function of family offices, and this includes organizing family meetings and supporting family and ownership councils. In addition, complex collective trusts require the ongoing preparation of family trustees, including those who interact with the board. In this model, voting trusts often provide the ownership link to the board and the business.

While this pattern of development is common in highly successful families, it is not the most common pattern in family business. Most families do not face such dramatic taxation issues. Their businesses do not grow to the same degree, and tax consequences do not lead to dramatic extraction of capital from the business. In this case, ownership dispersal is more common. An increasing number of individual shareholders hold smaller amounts of ownership over time. Some families create a hybrid model, by holding different classes of stock in different ways. Shares of voting stock are put in a trust, while shares of common stock are dispersed to individuals. But gradual dispersal is the most common form of ownership evolution, and this trend often leads to a particular pattern of governance development.

Most family businesses develop business and family governance in tandem, and their early boards start out functioning more like family or ownership councils. When families grow slowly or stock dispersal is delayed, it can be many decades before the controlling shareholders no longer sit together around the boardroom table. While the scale of the family ownership is small, the board tends to be composed of the company's largest shareholders, and it serves as an ownership forum. At this stage, there is often no separation of family and business governance, and neither practice is highly developed.

As the business grows and ownership disperses, there is an increasing need to develop practices focused on specific, separate functions. As the business changes scale, it requires the development of mature board practices. As the family disperses, ownership communication and consensus building cannot be done in the boardroom. As these functions become more complex, they tend to separate. Sometimes, this is a very gradual process, involving the incremental development of new practices, but often the creation of separate family governance is done in one dramatic leap.

The separation of family and business governance is often culturally traumatic. Historical models are lacking, and the change is often perceived as a departure from the past. In addition, some family owners naturally resist change, while others advocate strongly for it. The development of parallel governance practices can continue for long periods of time. Separating functions is confusing and often resisted. It seems to add complexity, and individuals often do not understand the new separation of roles. Often, family members are asked to give up long-held positions, and this can trigger feelings of personal loss. Board composition and the addition of independent directors are often thorny issues at this stage, as is the role of the family, inside and outside the business. Sometimes important business decisions need to be made in the midst of all this change, and resolving issues impacts the development process. The separation of governance functions can feel like the separation of the business and the family, rather than a step in the process of holding them together.

As parallel governance develops, practices often continue to change for long periods of time. Ongoing adaptation is common in the creation of effective processes for relating the business and the family. Over time, the board must develop mature business practices, and the family must create effective ownership practices. Family governance should include regular family meetings, and the development of family and ownership institutions like councils or assemblies. These new institutions should represent ownership and the family collectively, and provide an avenue for shareholder education and communication. Most critical of all, the family and business sides of governance must continue to relate directly to one another as they evolve. This can become a moving target on both sides, as they develop separate functions.

Organizing family ownership effectively

Family governance is less standardized than business governance. While models do exist, organizing large families is challenging and often requires ongoing adaptation over long periods of time. Creating a council, conducting effective large family meetings, and keeping people interested are all challenging goals that require an ongoing commitment. Trial and error is a necessary part of creating the right fit for the family and overall governance. To be effective, this fit has to reflect history and reinforce the culture and values of the family. Among the key issues to decide is who to include, and how they will participate. Are in-laws included? Is being a shareholder required? What is the family culture about representation and branches? What should the role of family managers or directors be in family governance? Each family needs to wrestle with these questions, come to solutions that reflect their culture, and then be willing to revisit the questions again.

Family governance can become very complex over time. More and more interrelated structures tend to be layered together, including trusts, family and ownership councils, foundations, and family offices. These are linked in a network of functions, and need to be coordinated with one another and aligned with the family business. The complexity of family governance is often driven by wealth creation, and supporting wealth management can be vital to the continuity of the family. On a larger level, the key objective of family governance is coordinating ownership's interaction with the business. This is the key to maintaining concentrated ownership control in large family groups and working with the board and management to optimize business performance.

Good family governance can take many forms, but its key function is to promote effective ownership communication and deliberation. Large family ownership groups need to be educated about the business, its history, and its current challenges. They need to understand the values, vision, and goals of the business and the family, and how these are related and support each other. Good family governance, however, needs to do more than provide information. It must enable ownership discussion and feedback. The family itself must make decisions, including fundamental decisions about how it will govern both itself and the business. Often, this requires ongoing family engagement and governance adaptation. Creating effective practices in family governance is quite challenging and active support from the board is often needed. Good leadership and a substantial investment are also required.

Family governance needs funding, and when no trust supports it, the company usually makes this an expense of shareholder relations. Business-funded family governance leads to regular family business meetings, and often includes the creation of family or ownership councils. Most often, these family governance institutions are representative and democratic. Members and leadership are usually elected, though some families prefer selection processes. Voting techniques vary, with some families voting by shares. Depending on the participation requirements, positions within family governance can be paid or voluntary. Sometimes compensation is based on a board model, with fees for meetings and for chairpersons. Most often, it is the leaders of family governance who are compensated for the significant amounts of time they contribute. Generally, expenses are paid for family members who participate in family governance activities.

The main function of family governance is to organize family meetings. These can include large annual assemblies, regular council meetings, educational seminars, meetings of foundation boards or trustees, and regular social events. Another common function of family governance is to produce regular newsletters or other communications. Many families also generate written policies, which can include family employment policies, codes of conduct, conflict resolution processes, and complex shareholder agreements. Family ownership can also guide the business by generating written policies that set shareholder value objectives, risk parameters and liquidity policy, or dictate board composition and director nominating processes. The most effective written policies begin by describing existing practices, so they are clear and any issues can be drawn out and resolved. Actual decision-making will always put written policies to the test, and good governors will continue to adapt and update their written policies in ways that reflect actual practice.

Another key function of family governance is aligning family ownership goals with current business strategy. Family owners need a high-level understanding of the strategy of the business and should support the level of reinvestment necessary for success. Family governance provides the means of educating the family about the business, its industry, its competitive position, and strategic goals. Family owners should understand how the company creates value for its customers and which industry trends are creating strategic challenges and opportunities. Family owners need to know about historic reinvestment levels, and understand how capital needs may change in relation to current strategies.

Effective ownership education allows family governance to deliver appropriate ownership feedback on strategy. Business strategy must fit the family's values and vision of ownership. Most often, this involves assuring that strategy is aligned with a well-articulated shareholder value proposition. The role of family governance is to deliver a clear, well-informed expression of ownership expectations regarding levels of reinvestment, risk, profitability, liquidity, and current shareholder distributions.

Fulfilling these functions of family governance can add a lot of value to the family business. To do so, however, they must be closely coordinated with the business and serve to build family cohesion and commitment. This takes a lot of work, resources, and engagement. The business and board must support the development of family governance, and the family must recognize its shared interests and renew its commitment to the business. Good family governance is the key to maintaining concentrated ownership control in large family ownership groups. When the family is united and its purpose clear, then even dispersed ownership can support the optimal development of the business.

Fulfilling the potential of concentrated ownership

Family businesses go through a natural evolution of development. Each business and family goes through its own unique process of growth, and must eventually confront the challenges of scale change. Often, these challenges are compounded by simultaneous, dramatic change in both the business and the family. Generational successions are the most fundamental drivers of change, and early family transitions often create fundamental transformations in both ownership and management. The resulting governance and ownership structures tend to define the ownership/business relationship and establish how the two sides of the system are organized and interrelate. Sustaining a symbiotic relationship between the family and its business is essential.

In family business, early governance practices tend to become well established and difficult to change. Often the business develops to a certain size and then scale change becomes more gradual. This can lead to an extended period where there is less pressure on governance to evolve. But, as the family grows and ownership is dispersed, a second dramatic transition becomes inevitable. With time, the family's controlling ownership moves out of management and the boardroom, and the family business must make the leap to parallel governance that is capable of renewing concentrated ownership control in a large, dispersed ownership group.

The need for parallel governance is inevitable in large family businesses. Both families and businesses tend to change scale exponentially over time. Success itself is a common driver of change, and the pace of change can be an indicator of business performance. To remain effective, governance must adapt to the emerging realities of the family business. Life cycles in the family and business will inevitably challenge the effectiveness of governance, and this causes many family businesses to become proactive about creating parallel governance.

The effective adaptation of parallel governance is challenging for families. It is especially important for the family to have clarity and consensus about decision-making processes and who holds decision rights. In making key decisions, however, consultation beyond narrow decision rights is often critical, and this is particularly true in relation to strategic decisions made by the board. Clarity about how ownership consultation is triggered and conducted is essential, as is a commitment to engagement through the processes put in place.

The main outcome of active consultation is the building of trust. A clear and consistent process of consultation helps solidify the appropriate separation of roles within governance. The management, board, and ownership should all share a common understanding of their separate roles and how they will interrelate. Active consultation leads to the regular re-examination and renewal of shared objectives. It places them in direct relation to current developments and decisions within the business. Creating clarity about roles and maintaining active consultation across the family business system are key components of enabling effective decision-making.

Families in business must reconcile the classic paradox of needing both stability and change. Inevitably, both the family and business face change, and their changes can compound one another. Without a strong stabilizing influence, the natural tendency of the system is to pull apart. Committed family ownership is the stabilizing core of a family business. Often, this commitment is based on a sense of stewardship and the historical foundation of the family's business vision and values. Good business performance is also critical to supporting this core commitment, as is the reasonable prospect of long-term, sustainable value creation. Ownership commitment is not cast in stone and must be constantly renewed in order to simultaneously maintain stability and pursue adaptive change.

The most successful business families focus on adapting good governance. They proactively pursue the clarification of roles and processes, and work to enable deliberation and alignment between ownership and its business. This, in turn, helps build trust across the system, which enables even the most challenging decisions and transitions to be executed successfully. Scale change complicates the goal of maintaining concentrated ownership control and enabling the family business's competitive advantage. As the system grows, achieving this goal becomes more challenging, and requires the proactive development of effective, parallel governance, and particularly good family governance. When conscientiously pursued and adapted over time, good parallel governance can help sustain concentrated ownership control, even in large family ownership groups. This, in turn, enables the family business to pursue strategies that maintain its competitive advantages and create optimal business performance.

12
Counterintuitive Insights

Colleen Lief and John L. Ward

Throughout this book, concepts that challenge accepted notions of family business practice and conduct have been examined. While the surprising conclusions are interesting in their own right, their real power lies in the insights that family firms can gain and that aid them in leveraging their uniqueness. Greater awareness of self and of the dynamics that can drive companies to robust performance may be the simplest yet most vastly overlooked dimension of enhanced family business success. Companies, like people, may instinctively turn to outside solutions to complex situations, when often the solution lies within a closely held universe. This tendency may be particularly hazardous to family enterprises, the origin and strength of which lies with the synchronous relationship between two bound, yet discrete parties – a founder and his business, the pioneer and the successor, the family and the business, the ownership and the management, the board and the family, the board and the business.

Conventional preconceptions and counterintuitive truths – selected summary

Professor Lorange started the discussion with an exploration of the primary issues threatening family business growth – the natural tilt toward kingdoms and silos and the necessity of developing internal entrepreneurs within the family enterprise. The evolution of a 'meeting place' culture, supporting an atmosphere of immediacy in decision-making and a keen attention to superior strategic planning are key to overcoming these potential pitfalls.

The chapter on unconventional strategy counters some of the most widely held erroneous beliefs about families in business. Nepotism, while practically universally regarded as something best avoided, was demonstrated to add value and depth to corporate management structures. A family successor not only knows the history, values and culture of the company, years of formal and informal teaching have imparted an 'idiosyncratic knowledge' to the next cadre of leaders. This tacit, inborn wisdom has been gleaned over years and generations of owner-managers' experiences.

Financial pundits criticize most family firms' underleveraged position. They see this as a waste of a valuable resource. Family businesses often avoid debt in an effort to retain control over their enterprises. The discipline inherent in living within a company's means endows a tight-fisted approach to capital investment decisions. Less capital means family firms resort to less capital-intensive and perhaps less risky strategies – or at least strategies that stray furthest from core values and enduring goals.

Top-notch strategic planning 'starts with the family.' This notion, in itself, seems counterintuitive when talking about the planning process of a commercial enterprise. However, nothing could be further from the truth.

A corporation owned by a family group has a special relationship with its owners that must be recognized and respected. The long-term, overarching purpose and goals of the company emanate from the needs, values and direction of the owning family. Further, drawing leadership from within family ranks, continuity and the maintenance of a guiding strategic vision are enhanced. While conventional wisdom says that the talent pool is limited by such an approach, family firms find that a stable, yet responsive, competitor emerges. Mixing family and business might appear to complicate matters needlessly. But family managers face an ever-growing ownership group that relies on corporate success for a sustained livelihood and are vociferous in their praise – and criticism, if cash flow is threatened. Since owners generally far outnumber family managers, they must be convinced of the strategy and direction of the business and feel free to challenge management assumptions and performance. Rather than acting as a distraction, family ownership provides the basis for strategic renewal, based on shared culture and values. Many families have found parallel planning, with convergence at several key intervals, helps dovetail the aims and needs of the company with its owners.

Several real world studies confirm what Professor Denison and Ms Lief suggest in their chapter – that family businesses generally perform better than non-family firms. This is surprising as both entrepreneurial tendencies and the concentration of personal wealth would be expected to stifle a family company's risk threshold and profitability. Both of these expectations remain unmet, as the longer-term investment horizon possible in family-owned enterprises allows different, distinct risk parameters. And, rather than lead to overly-conservative investment choices, individuals holding the majority of their personal wealth in the family business actually frees family managers to assume the level of risk right for the company. The success of both entrepreneurship and capital concentration is borne out by the outstanding performance already noted.

Family firms, on average, perform better than their non-family counterparts because a number of factors come together, in different proportions and potencies in different companies, to maximize the power of their natural uniqueness. (1) Family successors bear an intimate knowledge of the business and the philosophy of the founder. (2) As the candid reflection of one individual's thoughts, dreams and character, the inimitable nature of family companies becomes a real source of competitive advantage. (3) Families in business are concerned with more than making money. Their interests are not that narrowly defined and frequently include issues related to the community, environment, labor, religion, behaving with integrity. (4) Through many years of experience and a lifetime of learning, family members, and through them their firms, possess the agility to deftly manage competing aims and apparently disparate concepts. (5) Relatives act as trustees of family and corporate character by instituting thoughtful hiring and human resources policies, thus preserving the secret to their success for the next generations.

So much has been written about succession planning in family businesses that one would think that everything has been said. Professor Schwass finds that there may be too much emphasis on planning and not enough on the 20 plus years that come next. The family and business must rally around the successor to help insure the success of the transition to the next generation of leadership and ownership.

Contrary to expected norms, successors should assume an assertive posture in dealing with their relatives. New leaders must pay less attention to walking on eggshells and more on advancing the transition toward achievement. Through strident action and a definitive agenda, successors can 'break the deadlock between the generations.' In this way, they gather the respect and affirmation of family, management and directors and can spearhead the charge to the future.

Professor Kohlrieser demonstrates the fallacy of believing that conflict should be avoided at all costs. Many see conflict as a direct threat to family, and therefore business, harmony. But by 'putting the fish on the table,' family unity is much more likely to be preserved. While it seems improbable that family relationships would be healthier after confrontation than before, the real understanding and intimacy that can result from such authentic communication can bind wounds and mend fences.

It is also popular to believe that putting the perspectives of others at the top of the agenda is the best way to establish the rapport necessary to resolve problems. But, experience has shown that sharing one's own needs, fears and concerns first bears greater fruit. Being open with one's feelings shows a willingness to be vulnerable and takes great skill, both of which lead to better communication.

Following up on this thought, Professor Kahwajy counters the notion that family especially should run for the hills from potential disagreement. Unconscious beliefs and intentions can derail even those committed to finding a middle ground. What we do not know *can* hurt us. So through greater awareness of how much is behind our words, we have a better chance at the quality interactions and satisfying relationships that are so important to successful families and businesses.

Family constitutions are important. But, rather than focusing so sharply on the content of family constitutions, the process of developing the document should take precedence. Through a series of considered, inclusive steps, the right constitution is more likely to emerge. In this case, process is more important than product. The benefits of working together on this vital project are many and come from sharing and hearing each other's concerns and the feeling of commitment to the future that inevitably results. A fit appropriate to the family and business, self-awareness, melding the family's creativity toward insightful problem solving are far superior outcomes in writing a family constitution than anticipating every contingency.

While regulators and the public see the new governance rules as stemming the tide of corporate misbehavior, Professor Steger counters that other factors weigh more heavily on corporate comportment than new laws. It is appealing to think that morality could be pressed upon the world's large corporations. However, the character of the CEO, the stage in the business cycle, the competitive environment and its ownership form more commonly affect the way a business acts. Further, the world at large may think that family firms' advantage in aspiring to noble conduct lies in their often privately held status. Family businesses do have a predisposition toward better citizenship. Good governance flows from a connectedness to the past and an often rich history of living every day in accordance with principles and values.

Acknowledging their stature and global economic clout, enlightened commentators may opine that corporate governance is the same for family companies and that firms owned by families require the same qualities from their directors as non-family corporations. But family businesses are pursuing a rare breed in ensuring high levels of corporate accountability and performance – directors who too can balance the 'AND.' Directors on the boards of family-owned enterprises must at the same time remain dedicated to the family's heritage of values and feel compelled to challenge management. By doing both, outside directors become an indispensable value-added partner.

For family companies the nature of ownership is very differentiated. Owners are few and emotionally attached to each other and to their business. At the end of the day the owners have personal responsibility for the governance and conduct of the business. Family owners must learn the roles and competencies of good owners – subjects with no courses. They must be clear about their expectations as owners, yet respectful of the roles of executives and directors. Done well, owners add great value to the performance of their company.

It is hoped that coming face-to-face with these insights will spur serious thinking and lively discussion among family members as they chart the future course of their companies and act as standard-bearers of their founder's legacy. By questioning conventional wisdoms, family businesses have the opportunity to redefine what is possible and their own vision of success.

Index

Index compiled by Annette Musker